D0550644

H 57574

374

13/05/21

PSYCHOLOGY AND

This book is to be returned on or before
the last date stamped below.

19 APR 2004
03 DEC 2004
16 FEB 2005
15 NOV 2005
24 APR 2009
17 DEC 2010
24 NOV 2011

10 MAY 2012
30 MAY 2012
7 MAR 2013
10 JAN 2014

21 APR 1997
- 4 1997
11 MAY 1998
23 NOV 1998
30 NOV 1999
11 JAN 2000
11 JAN 2001
090501
16 NOV 2001
07 FEB 2002
2nd Sept 2002
31 OCT 2002

WITHDRAWN
CRAVEN COLLEGE

5723

CRAVEN COLLEGE

Craven College

07574

First published 1988
by Routledge
11 New Fetter Lane, London EC4P 4EE

Simultaneously published in the USA and Canada
by Routledge
29 West 35th Street, New York, NY 10001

Reprinted 1991, 1993, 1995

© 1988 Mark Tennant

Printed and bound in Great Britain by
Biddles Ltd, Guildford and King's Lynn

All rights reserved. No part of this book may be reprinted or reproduced
or utilized in any form or by any electronic, mechanical, or other means,
now known or hereafter invented, including photocopying and recording,
or in any information storage or retrieval system, without permission in
writing from the publishers.

British Library Cataloguing in Publication Data
A catalogue record for this book is available from the British Library

Library of Congress Cataloging in Publication Data
A catalog record for this book is available from the Library of Congress

ISBN 0-415-00560-4 (hbk)
ISBN 0-415-05032-4 (pbk)

CRAVEN COLLEGE

No th Yorks BD23 1JY

CONTENTS

Page

CONTENTS

EDITOR'S NOTE

The Routledge Series in International Adult Education brings to an English-speaking readership a wide overview of developments in the education of adults worlwide. Books are planned for the series of four different types:

a) about adult education in a single country
b) having a comparative perspective of two or more countries
c) having an international perspective
d) symposia of papers for different countries following a single theme.

This book has a theme that is relevant to adult education worldwide and therefore falls into the third category. It is a significant study because it addresses many of the issues in the psychology of learning from the perspective of an adult educator.

Mark Tennant is a lecturer in adult education in the Department of Adult Education, Sydney College of Advanced Education. He has published a number of articles on adult education in recent years and this study is an important addition to this international series of books on adult education.

Peter Jarvis
Series Editor.

LIST OF TABLES

LIST OF FIGURES

PREFACE

This book was written while I was a Visiting Fellow with the Department of Continuing Education at the University of Warwick in 1986. Many of the ideas grew out of lectures and seminars given to graduate students at the Institute of Technical and Adult Teacher Education, Sydney College of Advanced Education. These students were enrolled in one of a number of programs leading to an award in adult and continuing education. They comprised community educators, industrial and commercial trainers, aboriginal educators, ESOL teachers, literacy teachers, outreach workers, health education officers and so on. They were all practising adult educators who had completed undergraduate studies in psychology or a related discipline. This is the readership for whom this book will be most accessible - the graduate student who has a knowledge of psychology, and work experience in adult and continuing education.

The chapters are organised into three clusters of research and theory. The first of these focuses on theories which have a bearing on the affective aspects of adult learning and development (Chapters 2-4). The remaining clusters examine the role of cognitive factors in learning and development (Chapters 5-6) and the impact of the social context in which learning takes place. Apart from this, the sequencing of chapters is unimportant, and it is certainly possible to read them in any order.

It is a book about psychology and adult learning as opposed to being a book about the psychology of adult learning. The reader who wants a comprehensive account of psychology and its application to adult learning should look elsewhere. Similarly, the reader who wants an exhaustive treatment of any particular theory will not find it here. My approach has been to examine the seminal traditions of some key psychological theories and to discuss the issues and problems in applying them to an understanding of adult learning and development. I hope it will be useful for those who seek a critical understanding of psychological theory and research from the perspective of the adult educator.

I should like to express my gratitude to the following colleagues and friends who have made direct and indirect contributions to the book: Susan Roberts, who read the draft and made many helpful comments and suggestions; Chris Duke, who was my host at the University of Warwick; Rod McDonald and Keith Foster, who have supported and sustained the adult education programs at the Institute of Technical and Adult Teacher Education; and Peter Jarvis, who stimulated me to write the book and provided invaluable editorial guidance.

I am also indebted to the following publishers for permission to reproduce diagrams and figures:
1. Little, Brown and Company, for Tables 4.3 and 4.6 which appear in 'Adaptation to Life' by George E. Vaillant. Copyright 1977 by George E. Vaillant.
2. Croom Helm, for Table 82 which appears in 'Learning in Groups' by D. Jacques (1984).
3. Taylor and Francis, for allowing substantial excerpts from an article published in the International Journal of Lifelong Education to be used in Chapter 2. (Tennant, M 1986, Vol 5 No 2 pp 113-22)
4. Jossey-Bass, for Table 4.4 which appears in 'The Modern American College' by Arthur W. Chickering (1981).
5. The Open University Press for Tables 2.1 and 9.1 which appear in 'Adult Learning and Education' by Malcolm Tight (ed.) (1983).
6. The Writers and Readers Publishing Co-operative for Figure 9.1 which appears in 'Education: The Practice of Freedom' by Paulo Freire (1974).
I would also like to thank my immediate family who showed patience and understanding when I occasionally neglected my domestic duties.

Mark Tennant
Sydney, June 1987

Chapter One

INTRODUCTION

Existing approaches to understanding adult learning generally fall within one of three broad types. The first type seeks to provide a balanced overview of psychological theory and research together with an assessment of its relevance to adult education (eg. Knox, 1977; Lovell, 1980; Cross, 1982; Long, 1983). The emphasis is generally pragmatic: a description of various aspects of psychology is developed into an eclectic understanding of how adults best learn, this may be followed by a tentative list of principles to be adopted or procedures to be employed when teaching adults. There will usually be some comments about the conceptual ambiguities of a theory or the difficulties in verifying a particular research finding, but these are often parenthetical comments, set aside from the thrust of the text. A second type of approach to understanding adult learning is one which has a clearly articulated thesis and which uses psychological literature to support the thesis being proposed (eg. Knowles, 1978, 1984; Tough, 1979, 1982). Typically there is an attempt to identify and draw upon a selected set of psychological concepts and principles and thereby develop a programmatic (and sometimes prescriptive) statement about adult teaching and learning.

Neither of the above approaches leads to a critical understanding of the psychological theories in question. This is understandable, because when the agenda is clearly 'adult learning' rather than 'psychology', it appears cumbersome and unnecessary to address the conceptual and methodological problems of psychological theory and research. Nevertheless, failure to do so will mean that psychology will continue to be used in an uncritical way to support the normative rhetoric of adult

1

education.
  A third approach takes as its point of departure
a critical analysis of theory and research in adult
education and develops from this a view about adult
teaching and learning (eg. Griffin, 1983;
Brookfield, 1986). To date, instances of this type
have typically drawn upon a range of disciplines,
such as sociology, history, educational theory and,
of course, psychology. My purpose in writing this
book is to adopt the spirit of this approach, but to
orient it towards a focus on psychology as a
foundation discipline in adult education.
  In the chapters which follow then, I aim to
provide a critical account of those psychological
theories which have informed contemporary adult
education theory and practice. Each theory or body
of research is treated separately, in a separate
chapter, using two guiding principles. Firstly,
there is an attempt to provide a balance of
description, critique and comments on each theory's
influence on adult education. As far as possible I
have limited this process to those aspects of each
theory which are pertinent to the issues and
concerns of adult educators.
  Secondly, there is an emphasis on understanding
psychological development throughout the lifespan.
The reason for this is that the very notion of
'adult education' as a separate area of enquiry
implies that a distinction should be made between
adults and children. Moreover, it implies that
development and change is a feature of adult life
and that education has a continuing role to play in
the lives of all adults.
  In developing a critique of each theory I have
been mindful of Broughton's (1981:81) distinction
between different types and levels of critique. In
summary these are:

1. Theoretical critique - where conceptual
    weaknesses and internal contradictions within
    the theory are identified.
2. Empirical critique - where the adequacy of the
    theory is examined in the light of the evidence.
3. Practical critique - where the form, purpose and
    success of the practices promoted by the theory
    are assessed.
4. Ideological critique - where the sociological,
    historical and political origins, nature and
    consequences of the theory are analysed and
    evaluated.

An exhaustive critical analysis of a given theory
would require all four levels of critique. However,
in this book there is a mix of levels both within
and between the chapters. The aim is not to be
exhaustive, but to be selective and, for each
chapter only apply that level of critique which is
relevant to adult teaching and learning.

In spite of this apparent 'ad hoc' approach
there is a unifying theme which persists throughout
the text and which provides a framework linking the
different chapters. This theme concerns the nature
of the relationship between the person and the
social environment.

It is useful to think of the various
psychological theories addressed in the text as
deriving from one of two broad perspectives:
depending on whether they take the person or the
social environment as their point of departure.
Those theories which emphasise the primacy of the
person have a tendency to explain learning and
development in terms of the internal make-up of the
person. Thus the person is regarded as an entity
having some objective form which it is the
psychologist's task to discover, describe and
explain. This assumption implies that the person
has an integrity or autonomous dynamic which makes
it largely independent of the social environment.
In contrast, theories which emphasise the primacy of
the social environment have a tendency to explain
learning and development in terms of the external
forces impinging on the person. On this account the
person is reduced to the dependent position,
implying that the person can be explained and
understood as a product of social influences, at
least in all important respects.

This of course is an over-simplification and
most theories admit both internal and external
influences on learning and development. But
nevertheless, an emphasis on one or the other term
of the 'person-social environment' relation is
nearly always apparent. Within the person
perspective there is a tradition of research which
focuses on emotional development. In this
tradition, the emphasis is on how our concept of
self, and the conflicts within it, emerges and
develops as we proceed through the life course. The
groundwork in this tradition can be traced to the
humanistic psychology of Rogers and Maslow (Chapter
2), or to the psychoanalytic theory of Freud and its
subsequent developments (Chapter 3). Many of the
more recent theories of adult psychological

development borrow from both the psychoanalytic and humanistic traditions (eg. Loevinger, Gould, Levinson, Vaillant, Neugarten, Lowenthal). Adult educators have shown considerable interest in this research (eg. see Cross, 1982), mainly because it offers the prospect of providing a theoretical and research base for adult teaching and learning (Chapter 4). In particular, it provides us with a model of the end point of development, the 'fully functioning person' - the autonomous, independent and integrated adult personality - from which is derived a view about how adults learn best at various stages and phases of the life cycle (see Knowles, 1984; Tough, 1979; Allman, 1982; Weathersby, 1981). The other tradition within the person perspective is concerned with the person's knowledge and cognitive capacities. One area in this research attempts to explain the processes through which, in the course of our development, we attain an understanding of the world. The principal theorists and researchers in this area have been influenced by the seminal work of Piaget in the domain of cognitive development, and Kohlberg in the domain of moral development (Chapter 5). They have in common the mission of describing and explaining the sequence of stages which mark our progressive understanding of abstract concepts and moral regulations. Adult educators are interested in the extent to which we can talk of 'adult' cognitive stages, and whether the processes of stage progression are relevant to the processes of adult learning. Other research efforts have focused on measuring intellectual capacity over the lifespan or mapping individual differences in cognitive styles (Chapter 6).

The 'social environment' perspective encompasses a diverse range of theories and approaches. One class of approaches postulates a mechanistic relationship between the person and the social forces acting on it. On this account the person is a passive receiver of behaviours, roles, attitudes and values which are shaped and maintained by the social environment through rewards and sanctions. The most influential of these approaches is Skinner's stimulus - response psychology (behaviourism). His theory has had an impact on teaching and learning in all sectors of education. In adult education his legacy is most apparent in the importance attached by many adult educators to the need for setting behavioural objectives and providing regular feedback and reinforcement

(Chapter 7). This mechanistic approach is also apparent in some of the descriptive research on adult life phases (eg. Chickering and Havighurst, 1981).

An opposing class of approaches within the 'social environment' perspective postulates a more active role for the person in the person-society dialectic. Learning and development are thus seen as proceeding through a constant interaction between the developing person and the social environment. Both the developing person and the social environment are active in this process - this is why it is referred to as a dialectical process. In adult education this general approach is recognisable in the writings of Freire, Lovett, Griffin, Brookfield and others who draw attention to the working of social processes in shaping individual identity and the need for adult learners to resist forms of enculturation which are alienating and oppressive (Chapter 9).

The above distinctions are useful as a framework for locating different psychological theories - but they are more than this. In everyday life people adopt strong veiws on the relationship between person and society, and those views influence their perception of political, economic and moral issues. Let me illustrate this with some examples of an extreme person perspective, which is commonly manifested in the way people attribute to individuals the responsibility for events and actions which are more properly considered social phenomena. Thus we hear that the unemployed are lazy or inept (and could therefore enter employment if they changed their attitude or improved themselves), migrants are reprehensible for failing to learn their adopted country's language and the illiterate have only themselves to blame for their incomplete schooling (and should therefore pay fees as adult second-chance learners). A variant of this tendency to attribute to the individual more responsibility and control than is warranted, is the tendency to overemphasise the natural (biological) and unalterable aspects of the individual. Thus boys are seen as naturally different from girls (and by implication attempts to change this are futile); homosexuality is deemed to be unnatural (and therefore consensus cannot establish it as a legitimate lifestyle); and it is said that there are natural racial differences in intelligence (a view which challenges the efficacy of educational intervention). These few examples, which illustrate

5

a bias in allocating responsibility towards the individual, constitute a challenge to the wisdom or morality of collective responsibility and social intervention.

The tensions and conflicts found in the above examples from everyday life have their parallels in the adult education literature. They are particularly evident in some key issues in adult education such as the nature of self-directed learning, needs-based provision, equity and access, and the nature of the relationship between teachers and learners - issues which are informed by psychological theory and research.

In the text which follows I consider in more detail the above general scenario. I argue that many of the prevailing theories in psychology and adult education lead to an over-regular and over-systematic view of adult learning and development, which is best understood as a dialectical process subject to the vagaries of historical and social variation.

Chapter Two

HUMANISTIC PSYCHOLOGY AND THE SELF-DIRECTED LEARNER

Self-directed learning is one of those foundation
concepts in adult education which strengthen its
identity as a distinct field of practice and
enquiry. The term is constantly used in journals,
monographs and texts in adult education and has
featured in a number of national and international
policy documents. It evokes associations with a
cluster of terms such as 'learner-centredness',
'independent learning', 'self-teaching', 'autonomy',
'freedom' and 'needs-meeting', all of which are
enthusiastically embraced within the emerging ethos
of adult education.

Like most foundation concepts, 'self-directed
learning' is articulated in a way which allows
seemingly limitless interpretations of what it is
and how it should be applied. Perhaps the best
analysis of the concept to date is to be found in a
series of articles by Stephen Brookfield (1981,
1985a, 1985b, 1985c), who locates the origin of
self-directed learning in three distinct schools of
thought.

To the banner of self-directed learning can be
rallied those philosophers who advocate the
development in students of powers of critical
insight, independent thought and reflective
analysis. Hence, the injunctions of Paterson
and Lawson regarding the importance of using a
liberal arts curriculum or of emphasising in the
teaching of craft skills the cognitive, rational
and intellectual dimensions, are perfectly
consistent with an interpretation of a
self-directed learner as an individual skilled
in making judgements of the intellectual merit
of various theories, arguments or propositions.
Humanistically inclined adult educators can also

> claim philosophical kinship with the idea since
> it appears to be but an educational
> interpretation of the notion of
> self-actualisation. Indeed, adult educators
> such as Knowles and Tough, both of whom can be
> placed within the tradition of humanistic
> psychology, are the writers most associated with
> this concept. Finally, critical theorists of
> adult education such as Freire and Mezirow can
> also lay claim to the concept as one which
> neatly summarises the idea that adult education
> should be concerned to bring into the learner's
> critical consciousness those assumptions,
> beliefs and values which have been uncritically
> assimilated and internalised during childhood
> and adolescence.   (1985a:19)

The first of these schools of thought has been
labelled elsewhere (Darkenwald and Merriam, 1982) as
the 'cultivation of the intellect' approach, which
stresses the development of rational minds through a
teacher-centred and subject-focused curriculum. In
this approach the self-directed learner is
considered the ideal product of a very traditional
educational experience. As such, it is an approach
which is inimical to mainstream adult education
theory and practice. The remaining two schools of
thought, the 'humanistic' and the 'critical
awareness', have had a profound impact on the
struggle to define the goals, purposes and practices
of adult education. In particular they have
competing views concerning the nature, rationale and
purposes of self-directed learning. The 'critical
awareness' approach is treated in a later chapter –
the focus in this chapter is on the humanistic
approach.
    Self-directed learning is the centrepiece of
Knowles' model of the lifelong learner, who
possesses the following skills:

> The ability to develop and be in touch with
> curiosities (to engage in divergent thinking).
>
> The ability to formulate questions ... that are
> answerable through inquiry (to engage in
> convergent or inductive-deductive reasoning).
>
> The ability to identify the data required to
> answer the various kinds of questions.
>
> The ability to locate the most relevant and

reliable sources of data.

The ability to select and use the most efficient means for collecting the required data from the appropriate sources.

The ability to organize, analyze, and evaluate the data so as to get valid answers.

The ability to generalize, apply and communicate the answers to the questions raised.   (1972:163)

The adult educator has a responsibility to foster these skills, and the best way to do this, argues Knowles, is to adopt an andragogical approach to learning. The andragogical approach is characterised by a set of assumptions that the adult teacher has about the adult learner viz:

1.   There is a development of the self concept from dependency to self-direction.
2.   Adults have accumulated experiences and these can be a rich resource for learning.
3.   In children, readiness to learn is a function of biological development and academic pressure. In adults, readiness to learn is a function of the need to perform social roles.
4.   Children have a (conditioned) subject-centred orientation to learning, whereas adults have a problem-centred orientation to learning.
5.   For adults the more potent motivators are internal.

Using these assumptions as a starting point, Knowles proceeds to specify the skills, processes and techniques of helping adults learn. A key element in this is the learning contract, which is a device used by learners to guide and plan their learning. Typically, a learning contract requires some kind of diagnosis of needs, followed by a specification of goals and objectives, the identification of learning strategies and resources, and the evaluation of progress. In most applications of the learning contract method, the contract is negotiated between the learner and an adviser, who normally has a vested interest in the learning activities in the contract (eg. supervisor, peer, academic).
     This scenario for adult learning has been critically analysed by several commentators (Cross, 1982; Griffin, 1983; Jarvis, 1984; Hartree, 1984; Brookfield, 1985a; Tennant, 1986) who have

highlighted the gaps between theory and practice, the untenable nature of the andragogical assumptions, the lack of supporting evidence, its conceptual limitations, and its ideological impact. The remainder of this chapter expands some of these claims.

The view that adults are, or should be, self-directed learners, receives its support from three distinct sources:

1. Empirical work on the prevalence and nature of self-directed learning.
2. The influence of humanistic clinical psychology.
3. Theoretical and empirical work in the psychology of lifespan development.

Empirical studies

The best known empirical work on the nature and ubiquity of self-directed learning is to be found in Tough's (1967, 1968, 1979, 1982) investigations of the learning 'projects' of adults. A learning project is a major learning effort which is a deliberate and sustained (minimum 7 hours) attempt to gain some clear knowledge and skill. Using these criteria, Tough was able to show that the typical adult spends about 90 - 100 hours on each learning project, conducts eight such projects every year, and plans or directs the projects personally. A summary of his approach and findings is set out in Table 2.1.

To Table 2.1 can be added Tough's list of the key elements in self-directed learning viz:

1. knowledge and ability to apply the basic process of planning, conducting, and evaluating learning activities;
2. ability to identify one's own learning objectives;
3. ability to select the appropriate planning strategy and planner expertise;
4. ability to direct one's own planning when that course of action is appropriate;
5. ability to make sound decisions about the setting and time management of learning activities;
6. ability to gain knowledge or skill from the resources utilized;
7. ability to detect and cope with personal and situational blocks to learning;
8. ability to renew motivation;

Table 2.1:   The learning project.

---

1. A learning project (major learning effort):

    -   highly deliberate effort
    -   to gain and retain certain definite
        knowledge and skill
    -   clear focus
    -   at least 7 hours

2. Populations surveyed:

    A variety of groups (e.g. school teachers,
    parish ministers, unemployed, bank officers,
    factory workers) in a range of locations
    (e.g. Toronto, Vancouver, Nebraska, Kentucky,
    West Africa, New Zealand).

3. A middle or median person:

    -   conducts 8 different learning projects in
        one year
    -   spends a total of 700 hours altogether at
        them

4. Who plans the learning efforts from one session
    to the next?

    -   the learner: 68%
    -   a group or its leader-instructor: 12%
    -   a pro or friend in a one-to-one
        situation: 8%
    -   a nonhuman resource (records, TV, etc.): 3%
    -   mixed (no dominant planner): 9%

5. Out of 100 learning projects, 19 are planned by
    a professional educator and 81 by an amateur.

6. Most common motivation: some anticipated use or
    application of the knowledge and skill.

    Less common: curiosity or puzzlement, or
    wanting to possess the knowledge for its own
    sake.

    Rare (less than 1% of all learning efforts):
    credit.

Adapted from: Tough, 1983:142

7. ability to evaluate and receive feedback about
   progress.   (1978:197)

The elements identified here are certainly
compatible with the skills of self-directed learning
identified by Knowles (1973), which were quoted
earlier. In both accounts the self-directed learner
is one who masters a range of learning techniques
and processes.
     Another significant development in the empirical
investigation of self-directed learning has been the
construction of a diagnostic test, the Self Directed
Learning Readiness Scale (Guglielmino and
Guglielmino, 1982). This scale has the endorsement
of a number of prominent adult educators in North
America, including Chickering, Houle, Knowles and
Tough. Thus the items it contains can be considered
representative of the orthodox North American view
of self-directed learning.
     Once again, it is Brookfield (1985c) who has
pin-pointed the weaknesses of this research. He
argues that the structured interview schedules and
prompt sheets of Tough and the measurement scale of
the Guglielminos are inadequate in a number of
important respects. First, the people surveyed have
been primarily drawn from middle class,
educationally advantaged populations and thus
Brookfield remarks '... to talk of the adults' (in a
generic sense) propensity for self-directed learning
on the basis of research into samples comprised
chiefly of middle-class Americans is a dangerous act
of intellectual ethnocentrism. Very few researchers
have chosen to investigate the self-directed
learning activities of working class adults...
Conspicuous by their absence are studies of
self-directed learning among Blacks, Puerto-Ricans,
Hispanics, Asians or American Indians' (1985c:24).
A second point of criticism concerns the way in
which expectations play a role in influencing an
interviewee's recall of a learning experience. For
example, the finding by Tough that learning projects
often originate in an action goal, may be attributed
to the skills-oriented examples the interviewers use
when explaining the 'typical' learning project.
Thirdly, the use of questionnaires and scales
presupposes a familiarity with this form of data
gathering, a familiarity which cannot be assumed for
all groups in society. Finally, argues Brookfield,
there has been insufficient attention given to the
quality and worth (value) of the learning activities
reported. It is also instructive to note the

culture - specific nature of the Guglielmino items
which make no reference to group learning and appear
biased towards print material and middle class life
styles (e.g. libraries, personal responsibility for
learning, long term goals).

The claim then, that adults in the community are
largely self-directed learners - and that adult
educators should adapt to this reality by adjusting
their pedagogic practices and the nature of the
service they offer - is a claim which rests on
rather weak foundations.

Humanistic clinical psychology

The influence of humanistic psychology can be seen
in Knowles' conception of self-directed learning,
particularly in his endorsement of the term
'self-actualisation' and in his construction of the
ideal teacher-learner relationship.

The concern with the 'self' is a hallmark of
humanistic psychology, which emerged as a protest
against the scientific explanation of the person.
Scientific methods reduce the person to the status
of being an 'object' for scientific enquiry. By
contrast, humanistic psychology reaffirms the human
qualities of the person - such as personal freedom,
choice and the validity of subjective experience.
Among the self theorists in psychology perhaps the
most prominent names are Kurt Goldstein (1939), Carl
Rogers (1951), Gordon Allport (1961) and Abraham
Maslow (1968a). Maslow's work has had a
considerable range of application and so I will take
his view of self actualisation as the paradigm. He
presents his view as a theory of motivation.

In outline his theory is simple, he offers a
number of categories of motive which are related in
a hierarchy of prepotency. By this it is meant that
the person remains under the control of the motive
at the 'lower' level until the object of that motive
is achieved or its satisfaction assured. As soon as
this occurs the person comes under the sway of the
motive force at the next (higher) level. When and
only when this is satisfied the person becomes
subject to the next, and so on. A motive of a lower
level is always prepotent over one at a higher
level. The highest, which comes into operation only
when all other forces are quiescent, is called the
'need for self-actualisation'. The details of the
hierarchy are as follows:

Level 1. <u>Physiological needs</u> such as hunger, thirst

and sex, sleep, relaxation and bodily integrity. These must be satisfied before there come into play ...

Level 2. <u>Safety needs</u> which call for a predictable and orderly world, safe, reliable, just and consistent. While these are not satisfied the person will be occupied in attempts to organise his/her world so as to provide the greatest possible degree of safety and security. If satisfied, he/she comes under the forces of ...

Level 3. <u>Love and belongingness needs</u> which cause him/her to seek warm and friendly human relationships.

Level 4. <u>Self-esteem needs</u> - the desire for strength, achievement, adequacy, mastery and competence, for confidence in the face of the world, independence and freedom, reputation and prestige.

Level 5. <u>Self-actualisation</u> - the full use and exploitation of talents, capacities and potentialities. Self-actualisers are able to submit to social regulation without losing their own integrity or personal independence; that is, they may follow a social norm without their horizons being bounded in the sense that they fail to see or consider other possibilities. They may on occasion transcend the socially prescribed ways of acting. Achieving this level may mean developing to the full stature of which they are capable.

The way Maslow specifies the relationships between levels in the hierarchy exposes him to some forceful criticisms. The first concerns the claim that if one has satisfied lower needs (and not otherwise) one will necessarily proceed to the higher steps on the ladder. By deduction, those who have had their every physiological and safety need satisfied throughout life will inevitably become those who develop their highest potentialities. Those who have suffered long continued deprivation of physiological and safety needs will have had little opportunity to develop their higher levels. In plain words, those raised in relative luxury will become more creative, original and integrated personalities, those raised in disadvantageous circumstances will end up as inferior products. Facts do not seem to bear this out and exceptions come too readily to mind. It is patently untrue that one must attend to the lower levels before the higher. Fugitives are not compelled to defer further attemps to evade their enemies until they have satisfied their need for food; not even if they are at the point of starvation. One is not compelled to attend to safety needs before pursuing love and belongingness. Danger often brings out strong propensities for loving, as in times of war or pestilence. Martyrs have pursued what can only be called self-actualisation under the certainty of death.

In addition to these objections concerning the relationship between levels in the hierarchy, there are some shortcomings in the way Maslow has conceptualised Level 5 in the hierarchy, self-actualisation.

It appears that to be 'self-actualised' is to be psychologically healthy, to make full use of one's talents, capacities and potentialities. It is a 'need' or 'direction' the person strives towards to achieve psychological growth. In Maslow's words, once we have achieved a certain level of maturity we 'are motivated primarily by trends to self-actualisation (defined as on-going actualisation of potentials, capacities and talents, as fulfilment of a mission (or call, fate, destiny or vocation), as a fuller knowledge of, and acceptance of, the person's own intrinsic nature, as an unceasing trend towards unity, integration or synergy within the person)' (1968a:25). Self actualisers are said to have a 'superior perception of reality'; 'increased acceptance of self, of others and of nature'; and increase in 'problem-centring'; increased 'autonomy'; a greater 'freshness of appreciation' and 'richness of emotional reaction'; and a host of other qualities. The complete picture of the self-actualised person remains elusive, nevertheless it is something, we are told, towards which we are propelled. This tendency is not under deliberate, conscious control; rather it is a constituent part of our physiological endowment; it is something which characterises us as uniquely human. What Maslow would appear to be saying, then, is that humans are 'set' to self-actualise by virtue of their physiological make-up just as a sunflower seed is 'set' by its make-up to grow into a plant and produce a flower. Environmental conditions will make a difference to the result but the person is basically a persistent developer of its potential.

Knowles' adopts this view of psychological

growth in his attempt to construct a model for
helping adults to learn.

> ...the problem is that the culture does not
> nurture the development of the abilities
> required for self-direction, while the need to
> be increasingly self-directing continues to
> develop <u>organically</u>. The result is a growing
> gap between the need and ability to be
> self-directing. (1978:55)

The practices Knowles advocates are designed to
narrow this gap so that the learning processes of
adults are congruent with their need for
psychological growth.

The main difficulty with Knowles' andragogical
model (and its corollary, the learning contract) is
that it can be interpreted in a number of ways; as
an initial guide to assist adult learners towards
self-direction; as a process of learning appropriate
for adults who have already attained the capacity to
be self-directed, or as a means through which
individual needs can be reconciled with
institutional or organisational demands. The first
interpretation requires the assumption that adults
are, in fact, <u>not</u> self-directing and that they need
to be weaned away from traditional educational
consumption. Those who subscribe to this view
caution us against the too abrupt introduction of
self-directed learning; they argue that this type of
learning should be the goal of adult education
rather than its starting point. Not surprisingly
the reasons for a stance such as this may be quite
disparate, ranging from a paternalistic and
manipulative attitude to adult learners, through to
a genuine concern with providing supports for
self-directed learning efforts. Knowles certainly
acknowledges the importance of building a bridge
towards self direction '... adult educators have
been devising strategies for helping adults make the
transition from being dependent learners to being
self-directed learners' (1984:9) and he advises that
the andragogical model should be applied
selectively, as the situation permits, but this
interpretation is at odds with the thrust of his
thinking.

The second interpretation assumes that
self-directed learners have the capacity to control
and plan the content and processes through which
they learn. Ironically though, while adult
educators are admonished by Knowles for structuring

the content of a course, they are praised and given guidance for structuring the processes to be followed in a course. But why should self-directed learners follow the processes advocated by Knowles? Surely the imposition of a process can be just as restrictive and alienating as the imposition of content? Many adult students report being alienated by pre-structured self-assessment forms, particularly the 'objective' check-list variety. Also, the formal learning contract, particularly when it requires the specification of behavioural objectives, can often hinder rather than assist learning (Tennant, 1985a).

Knowles seems to regard the learning contract process as somehow neutral, he thus fails to acknowledge that it contains assumptions about the nature of knowledge and knowing; and consequently these assumptions remain unexplored by him. At best, he offers a truncated version of self-direction: the student directs the content, the educator directs the process.

The third interpretation above, that the learning contract is a means of reconciling individual needs with organisation goals, is another illustration of Knowles' diminished self-directed learner. It is unreasonable to expect individual needs, at all times, to be in harmony with organisational goals, and in instances of conflict individual needs may well be compromised. This prospect raises a still more fundamental question, is the learning contract a tool for learning or a tool for educators, trainers and managers? In a revealing section of 'The Adult Learner : A Neglected Species', Knowles advocates a pragmatic approach towards the use of learning theories by trainers and adult educators. Following a description of a range of learning theories, he outlines a number of criteria we should apply before selecting one theory over another. These criteria include: '...how does the proposed theory fit your organisation's management philosophy?' (1978:100) and 'Another thing to check before choosing a single theory is its congruence with the organisation's long-range development goals' (1978:10). Thus Knowles' attitude towards the different learning theories is based on the view that they are merely 'products' to be consumed and disposed of at will. This is a questionable view because it takes no account of the explanatory force of the theories concerned.

The organisation looms large in Knowles'

'Andragogy in Action'; testimony to this is the
following orientation address for new employees at
Lloyds Bank of California:

> 'You are entering an adult learning
> environment. This is a very participative
> process. We realise that you are interested in
> a career rather than just a job. We will help
> you become aware of the skills and knowledge you
> will need on your growth path with us. We will
> expect you to participate in certain training at
> each step ... We will expect you to use your
> training as an opportunity and gain from it the
> information you need for your own competence and
> future career growth. Your test will be on the
> job. If you are able to carry out your
> functions competently as a result of training,
> then your manager will recognize this and
> consider it in growth appraisals. If you fail
> to take advantage of the resources offered, then
> you will not become competent, not progress and
> probably not be with us in the future' (cited in
> Knowles 1984:75).

Is this an example of 'mutual respect',
'collaborativeness', 'mutual trust',
'supportiveness', 'pleasure', 'humanness', 'mutual
planning' and 'needs diagnosis' that Knowles refers
to earlier in this volume?
   Knowles' model for the ideal teacher-learner
relationship strongly reflects the counsellor-client
relationship in humanistic clinical psychology.
Both Rogers and Maslow were clinical psychologists
who normally dealt with individual clients, and who
were concerned with the psychological health of
these clients. It is not surprising then, to find
that the educational practices they advocate mirror
their clinical or therapeutic techniques. This is
well illustrated by Rogers' conception of the
teacher as a facilitator of learning. The qualities
of a good facilitator include:

1. <u>Realness and genuineness:</u>
   'When the facilitator is a real person, being
   what she is, entering into a relationship with
   the learner without presenting a front or
   facade, she is much more likely to be effective
   ... It means that she is being herself, not
   denying herself'. (1983:122-22)
2. <u>Prizing, acceptance and trust:</u>
   ' think of it as prizing the learner, prizing

her feelings, her opinions, her person. It is a
caring for the learner. But a non-possessive
caring. It is an acceptance of this other
individual as a separate person, having worth in
her own right. It is a basic trust - a belief
that this other person is somehow fundamentally
trustworthy'. (1983:124)
3. Empathic understanding:
    '...the ability to understand the student's
    reactions from the inside ... a sensitive
    awareness of the way the process of education
    and learning seems to the student'. (1983:129)

The emphasis on the personal relationship between
the facilitator and the learner is a feature of
Knowles' conception of the andragogical teacher who
'... accepts each student as a person of worth and
respects his feelings and ideas ... seeks to build
relationships of mutual trust (and) exposes his own
feelings' (1978:77-9). This is not the complete
picture, and Knowles adds to these qualities other
'principles of teaching' which build on this
relationship and encourage the learner to diagnose
needs, set objectives, enter contractual
arrangements and evaluate outcomes. It is
interesting that these additional principles of
andragogical teaching are similar to the strategies
adopted by those psychologists who seek to encourage
behaviour modification through self-direction. The
use of 'well defined objectives', 'contractual
agreements' and 'objective records of behavioural
changes' are all seen as essential to a successful
program of behavioural change (See Bandura, 1969,
and a summary in Knowles, 1978:88-9).
    It appears that Knowles' andragogical teacher
has been constructed from the techniques and
practices of psychologists working in two quite
different and opposing therapeutic traditions (the
humanistic and behavioural traditions). The
learning model which emerges leads to an unpalatable
view of education as the identification and
elimination of deficits or 'gaps' in knowledge,
performance, or self concept. For example, one
principle of andragogical teaching cited by Knowles
is 'The teacher helps the students identify the life
problems they experience because of the gaps in
their personal equipment'. Statements such as these
locate the source of 'life problems' away from the
institution and towards the individual with the
'solutions' being firmly implanted in the
teacher/taught relationship.

A second problem with the deficit model of
education relates to the diagnosis of 'deficits'.
Knowles makes it clear that deficits (and therefore
needs) are diagnosed not only by the learner, but
also by interests external to the learner: 'the
teacher involves the students in a mutual process of
formulating learning objectives in which the needs
of the students, of the institution, of the teacher,
of the subject matter and of the society are taken
into account'. (1978:78). But what should the
teacher do when there is a conflict of interests?
Clearly the conflict will be resolved according to
the distribution of power and status among the
various interests and the students can be expected
to fare poorly indeed. In this way the idea of
'diagnosing needs' will become yet another mechanism
for legitimating existing conceptions of worthwhile
education.
     One final point concerns the emphasis on
maintaining goodwill with the client (in therapy) or
learner (in teaching). In general, this is
desirable, but if goodwill means that conflict is
suppressed or avoided, then it may not always be
desirable. One reason for this is that conflict may
well stimulate and assist learning, and this view
can be supported both theoretically (Piaget, 1978)
and emipirically (Mugny and Doise, 1978). Another
reason for avoiding the emphasis on goodwill is that
it tends to become mandatory for both the adult
teacher (as an andragogue) and the adult learner (as
an andragogee). The effect of this on group
behaviour is that conflict is suppressed much more
and for longer than would normally be the case and
the result can be catastrophic. The point being
made is that a preoccupation with goodwill (ie.
goodwill = good teacher = good student) can do more
harm than good; and that conflict should be seen as
a natural and desirable outcome of the interaction
of two or more enquiring and challenging minds.

Lifespan development and the difference between child and adult learners

The literature on lifespan development will be
treated in a later chapter. For the present I wish
to return to the assumptions that Knowles' says are
the mark of the true adult educator. Because
Knowles considers that the assumptions of andragogy
are increasingly more appropriate as children
mature, his theory contains within it a view about
human development. Is this view reasonable?

Assumption 1
There is a development of the self concept from
dependency to self-direction (1978:55; 1984:9).
    Characterising the child as dependent and the
adult as independent does not seem problematic.
However, it becomes problematic when the question is
posed: dependent/independent with respect to what?
Children are obviously dependent on adults for many
things, but are they dependent learners? Everyday
observation confirms that children are remarkably
independent in their learning. Moreover, they are
quite innovative in the learning processes they
employ: fantasy, imagination, simulation, role play,
experimentation, games, and so on. One might even
suspect that adults need to be re-taught the
processes of self-direction, having lost them in the
years intervening between early childhood and
maturity. However, it must be conceded that young
children are not 'self-directed' in Knowles' use of
the term (diagnosing needs, setting objectives,
etc). But this is not to say that they are
dependent learners, quite the contrary, learning for
them is an activity which is natural and
spontaneous. It simply does not follow that because
children develop from dependence to independence in
some respects that they do so in all respects, and
it is a mistake to assume that children are
dependent learners while adults are independent
learners.

Assumption 2
Adults have accumulated experiences and these can be
a rich resource for learning. (1978:56; 1984:10)
    This assumption leads Knowles to advocate the
use of experience as a resource for learning and the
employment of experiential learning techniques.
However, I would argue that all learning should make
use of existing experiences, irrespective of their
degree and kind. As such, experience may well be a
characteristic that sets children apart from adults,
but it is not a characteristic which is relevant in
distinguishing between good educational practice for
adults and good educational practice for children.

Assumption 3
In children, readiness to learn is a function of
biological development and academic pressure. In
adults, readiness to learn is a function of the need
to perform social roles. (1978:57; 1984:11)
    It is difficult to see how this assumption has
any implication at all for the process of learning,

let alone for how this process should be
differentially applied to adults and children. The
only implication is that the <u>content</u> of what is
learned should be relevant to the learner's needs.
Apart from this, the assumption seems questionable;
children also have a need to perform social roles
and to adjust their behaviour to different social
settings; and adults, it can be argued, retain the
'biological' imperative to learn (ie. curiosity,
exploration, creativity for seemingly no immediate
purpose) and this is an important aspect of their
'readiness' to learn.

Assumption 4

Children have a (conditioned) subject-centred
orientation to learning, whereas adults have a
problem-centred orientation to learning. (1978:58;
1984:11)

Knowles does not present this distinction as a
'natural' difference between adults and children,
presumably if children were not conditioned to be
subject-centred they would 'naturally' be
problem-centred (e.g. infants). If this were the
case then organising educational activities around
problems would be equally applicable to children <u>and</u>
adults. If the advantages of the problem-centred
approach are accepted then surely children should be
'deconditioned' towards this approach. Once again
the assumption does not lead inevitably to a
differential learning process for adults and
children. Implicit in this assumption is the claim
that adults require immediate application of their
learning while children do not. While it may be
true that school curricula are geared towards the
postponed application of knowledge, this implies
nothing about the way in which children are
motivated to learn. I suspect that immediate
application is as relevant for children as it is for
adults. If anything, adults have a greater capacity
to tolerate the postponed application of knowledge,
partly because they conceptualise time in larger
'chunks' than children, and partly because they have
a capacity for hypothetical thinking (ie. thinking
about future possibilities) not evident in young
children.

Assumption 5

Regarding motivation to learn – the andragogical
model predicates that the more potent motivators are
internal (1984:12)

Internal motivators are those concerned with

self esteem, the need for recognition, self confidence and self-actualisation. Like the previous assumption this distinction between adults and children is not seen as 'natural': 'children and youth are naturally more motivated by intrinsic rewards than by external pressures, it is schools that have conditioned them to be otherwise'. (1984:13)

This assumption sits awkwardly with the view, stated earlier, that adults' readiness to learn is the result of the need to perform (externally imposed) social roles and that adults have a problem-centred (utilitarian) approach to learning. Notwithstanding this, Knowles needs to explain in more detail the distinction between 'internal' and 'external' motivators, their relationship with one another, their relevance to differences between adults and children, and the implications for educational practice. As it stands, the proposition that internal motivators become more salient with maturity has no support in the literature on lifespan developmental psychology.

The above criticisms rest largely on a particular interpretation of Knowles, one that links child learning with pedagogy and adult learning with andragogy. While Knowles is careful to avoid this extreme position, he must maintain some version of it in order to link andragogy with 'modern principles of adult learning', which is the hallmark of his work.

In this chapter I have argued that the rationale and empirical support for the humanistic concepts of self development and self-direction has gaps and weaknesses which need to be acknowledged. There is a need to distinguish the rhetoric of adult education from its rationale and empirical base. The prevailing rhetoric asserts that in everyday life adults are basically self-directed and that this self-direction is rooted in our constitutional make-up, it also asserts that self development is an inexorable process towards higher levels of existence, and finally it asserts that adult learning is fundamentally (and necessarily) different from child learning. These assertions should not be accepted as articles of faith.

Chapter Three

THE PSYCHOANALYTIC APPROACH

The work of Freud has had an overwhelming impact on
the development of twentieth century social
science. Its legacy is evident in contemporary
psychology, sociology, anthropology, linguistics,
literature, the arts, film and education. Its
legacy is more than historical, and familiarity with
the issues, methods and substantive content of
Freudian psychoanalysis is indispensable for anyone
with an interest in elucidating the human mind.
Freud provides us with a language for understanding
the person in everyday life, a language which is
based on a total conception of the person and not
some compartmentalised version of it. Perhaps this
accounts for his appeal to both the academic and
popular imagination.

Freud's writing is very accessible in the sense
that his style is exceptional and his ideas unfold
in a natural fashion (he received the Goethe Prize
for literature in 1930) but, paradoxically, the
totality of his thought is extremely elusive.
Reasons for this are easy to find: the sheer volume
of his published material, the evolution of his
thought over a span of fifty years and the fact that
he did not have a consistent position. All this
makes it very difficult to provide a systematic
account of Freud's work, let alone a thorough
critique. Short textbook accounts invariably do an
injustice to the complexities of psychoanalysis and
they risk confirming incorrect hearsay knowledge
about the subject (for example, that all little boys
want to have sex with their mothers, or that we are
all motivated by sex only).

Freud himself tried on a number of occasions to
set out his theories systematically, notably in the
publications 'Introductory Lectures on
Psychoanalysis', 'New Introductory Lectures on

Psychoanalysis' and 'Outline of Psychoanalysis'.
But even these are incomplete because they lack the
detailed, rich observations present in many of his
other publications. Freud has been criticised from
every conceivable angle, there are claims that his
theory is the product of a neurotic, distorted mind;
that its status as a science is questionable; that
he was unable to free himself from the cultural
milieu of his time (particularly in his views on
female identity); that because his work is largely
based on psychopathology, generalisations to the
normal population do not hold; and that his
psychotherapeutic technique simply doesn't work.
For the most part the debate on these, and other
closely allied issues, remains unresolved.

Psychoanalysis is notably absent from the
literature on adult teaching and learning. This is
difficult to understand, especially given the
importance adult educators attach to the emotional
climate of the classroom and the anxieties, fears
and hopes of learners. Indeed, there are several
ways in which adult educators can profitably
approach Freudian psychoanalysis:

1. As a source of clinical insight into the
    relationships among learners and between
    teachers and learners.
2. As a forceful theory which links individual
    identity with the way in which society is
    organised.
3. As a reference point for understanding
    psychoanalytic approaches to adult development.

Clinical insight and adult learning

Freud felt compelled to assume the existence of the
unconscious. He did so for a number of reasons,
which can best be understood in the context of his
experiences as a physician in Vienna in the late
nineteenth century. Freud became a close
professional associate of Joseph Breuer who had a
patient (Anna 'O') who exhibited the classical
symptoms of hysteria. These included physical
malfunctions such as partial paralysis, vomiting,
disturbances of sight and speech which could not be
traced to organic causes, in addition to a host of
other symptoms such as confusion, feelings of
helplessness and perceived worthlessness. The
medical profession at the time found it difficult to
know how to treat such cases. One commonly applied
treatment entailed the use of hypnosis. As a

phenomenon, hypnosis had attracted Freud. He had
studied with Charcot and others for a brief time in
Paris and was impressed with their demonstrations.
Two hypnotic phenomena were particularly salient for
Freud, these were: firstly, post-hypnotic suggestion
and secondly, the apparent ability of people to
recapture, under hypnosis, otherwise forgotten
memories. Later he wrote about post-hypnotic
suggestion:

> The well-known experiment, however, of the
> 'post-hypnotic suggestion' teaches us to insist
> upon the importance of the distinction between
> conscious and unconscious ..... a person is put
> into a hypnotic state and is subsequently
> aroused. While he was in the hypnotic state,
> under the influence of the physician, he was
> ordered to execute a certain action at a certain
> fixed moment after his awakening, say half an
> hour later. He awakes, and seems fully
> conscious and in his ordinary condition, he has
> no recollecton of his hypnotic state, and yet at
> the pre-arranged moment there rushes into his
> mind the impulse to do such and such a thing,
> and he does it consciously, though not knowing
> why.   (1958:261)

Thus the phenomenon of post-hypnotic suggestion
implies that we can be motivated by something of
which we are unaware. Moreover, the observation
that people under hypnosis remember previously
forgotten events, strengthens the proposition that
not all mental life is accessible to conscious
awareness. If one accepts the legitimacy of the
unconscious then much of Freud's corroborating
evidence and theoretical elaboration falls into
place quite neatly.
   The question of the relationship between the
conscious and unconscious was crucial for Freud, and
once again we find him looking to hypnosis for the
initial clues:

> When, in 1889, I took part in the
> extraordinarily impressive demonstrations by
> Liebeault and Bernheim at Nancy, I witnessed the
> following experience among others. If a man was
> put into a state of somnambulism, was made to
> experience all kinds of things in a
> hallucinatory manner, and was then woken up, he
> appeared at first to know nothing of what had
> happened during his hypnotic sleep .... But

> Bernheim brought urgent pressure to bear on him,
> insisted that he knew it and must remember it.
> And, lo and behold! the man grew uncertain,
> began to reflect, and recalled in a shadowy way
> one of the experiences that had been suggested
> to him, and then another piece, and the memory
> became clearer and clearer and more and more
> complete .... (1973a:132)

In his efforts to promote the recall of hypnotic
experiences, Bernheim demonstrated the permeability
of unconscious memory. This was important for Freud
because it meant that, at least in principle, the
unconscious was accessible to the conscious person.
It remained for Freud to identify the importance of
the unconscious in psychic life, how it operates and
how to gain access to it. His own assessment of his
contribution is testimony to the centrality of the
unconscious 'What I discovered was the scientific
method by which the unconscious can be studied'
(quoted in Jahoda, 1977:16).
Initially Freud used hypnosis to bring to the
surface the hidden, or forgotten, or unrecognised,
thoughts and feelings of his patients. Breuer's
earlier work with Anna 'O' had demonstrated the
benefits of hypnosis, especially when she was able
to express the strong emotions which these forgotten
thoughts had induced in her. But Freud finally
abandoned hypnosis because of his conviction that at
the heart of the therapeutic process was the
relationship between the patient and the therapist.
The core of this relationship is the phenomenon of
'transference' whereby the patient transfers on to
the therapist the intense feelings previously
associated with parents and other authority figures:

> We mean a transference of feelings on to the
> person of the doctor, since we do not believe
> that the situation in the treatment could
> justify the development of such feelings. We
> suspect, on the contrary, that the whole
> readiness for these feelings is derived from
> elsewhere, that they were already prepared in
> the patient and, upon the opportunity offered by
> the analytic treatment, are transferred on to
> the person of the doctor. (1973a:494)

Psychoanalysis hinges around the phenomenon of
transference. Patients are encouraged to work
through their transference feelings and the
therapist identifies the real life triggers of these

feelings. Thus it is crucial for the therapist to remain neutral with no social contact, otherwise real and neurotic feelings towards the therapist will be mixed.

The feelings expressed by the patient toward the therapist, together with the associations they trigger in the patient's mind, are the clues to unravelling the meaning of the patient's symptoms. In this way the analyst can identify repressed material and bring it to consciousness. In a passage from the case study of Dora, Freud remarks:

> He that has eyes to see and ears to hear may convince himself that no mortal can keep a secret. If his lips are silent, he chatters with his fingertips; betrayal oozes out of him at every pore. And thus the task of making conscious the most hidden recesses of the mind is one which is quite possible to accomplish.   (1953:77-8)

Psychoanalysis is thus an interpretive art based upon establishing connections between the recall, associations, feelings and symptoms of the patient. A fundamental principle is that nothing in mental life occurs randomly and that meaning can be found in the apparently trivial, (such as a slip of the tongue) the bizarre (such as a compulsion to wash one's hands fifty times a day) and the commonplace (recalling number 46 as 64). Patients are thus encouraged to report whatever comes to their mind, no matter how trivial or embarrassing.

Freud discovered that when patients gave free expression to each and every thought that occurred to them they often recounted traumatic sexual experiences which occurred during childhood. There was a time when he thought that neurosis in adults could be traced to childhood sexual encounters. He then found that the reluctance of his patients to describe these incidents, and the vague and unsatisfactory manner in which they did so, indicated that they were fabricated. They were not actual events, rather, they were the fantasies and wishes of his patients. Freud reasoned that these fantasies and wishes were caused by forces of a kind capable of accounting for their sexual tinge. This force, or energy, he called libido, which is a broadly conceived sexual energy. One should remember that by 'sexuality' Freud meant a kind of kinesthetic pleasure to be derived from bodily stimulation. From this notion followed the idea that sexual energy is directed at different bodily zones in the course of psychological development, which led to the well known psychosexual stages: the oral, anal, phallic and genital, and the celebrated Oedipus complex. The significance of these stages is twofold. Firstly, there is a difference between the way males and females negotiate the course of psycho-sexual development, a difference which accounts for male and female adult identity. Secondly, there is the more general argument that if the libido is blocked or frustrated at any stage, the outcome will be an indelible mark on adult personality. For example, if an infant is deprived of oral satisfaction (sucking) a portion of the libido will become fixated at this stage and subsequently expressed in adult behaviour (e.g. excessive eating or smoking). Thus many facets of adult behaviour can be understood in terms of infantile wishes and frustrations.

If we accept Freud's view that earlier childhood experiences are often evoked by situations which resemble the past, then it is easy to see how the adult teaching - learning situation can become fraught with emotional turmoil. Many of the anxieties expressed by adult learners can be construed as having their roots in childhood and infancy. This can be illustrated by considering some of the common expectations held about teachers. Salzberger-Wittenberg, et al (1983) outline five such expectations:

1. The teacher as the source of knowledge and
    wisdom.
2. The teacher as a provider and comforter.
3. The teacher as an object of admiration and envy.
4. The teacher as a judge.
5. The teacher as an authority figure.

The argument is that each of these expectations are associated with childhood feelings, especially towards the parents. In their extreme form they represent hopes or fantasies which can never be fulfilled. The anxiety associated with them, and the inevitable disappointment, will find expression in some way - usually as a transference of hostility and other feelings towards the teacher. The following passage refers to the expectation that a teacher is both 'provider' and 'comforter':

Teachers like others in helping professions, such as e.g. doctors, nurses, psychiatrists and

> social workers, easily become objects of
> infantile hopes: someone who will magically cure
> pain, take away frustration, helplessness,
> despair, and instead provide happiness and the
> fulfilment of all desires. We must expect that
> a person who holds on to the belief that such
> wishes should and can be met will easily feel
> disappointed, may soon turn away from us in
> anger, blame us for being totally unhelpful and
> seek out someone who appears more likely to
> comply with his wishes. What is so dangerous in
> this attitude, and our tendency to fit in with
> it, is that it is anti-development, for as long
> as there is a persistent belief that the
> individual does not have to struggle with some
> frustration and mental pain he is not likely to
> discover or develop any latent strengths.
> (Salzberger-Wittenberg et al, 1983:28)

The teacher too will bring to the classroom a set of
expectations, fears and aspirations, and it is
important to distinguish between those that are
based on unworked-over childhood conflicts and those
based on positive learning and childhood
experiences. Among other things, teachers fear
criticism, hostility and losing control - all these
are realistic fears and there is an ever-present
danger that the teacher's response will be infantile
(e.g. refusing to admit an error, becoming overly
apologetic and self-effacing about a small
mishandling of an event, not being able to criticise
students' work, attacking students). Once again,
Salzberger-Wittenberg (et al) supply a nice
illustration:

> (Teaching)... may stimulate the infantile
> aspects of our own personality. If the teacher
> has not sufficiently worked through these, he
> may become identified with the pupil's demand
> that all his desires should be fulfilled and
> endlessly gratified. The teacher may, for
> instance, agree that students need
> 'spoon-feeding' and thus be inclined to do most
> of the work for them. He may not realise that,
> in acceding to their infantile wishes, he is not
> only pampering them and undermining their innate
> capacities, but at the same time satisfying his
> own wish that learning should be easy. Equally,
> a teacher who has been, or longed to be, his
> parents' special child may gain vicarious
> satisfaction when he bestows special attention

on his favourite pupil. (The rest of the class
will have to suffer the pangs of jealousy which
the teacher has never been able to cope with
adequately). These modes of behaviour encourage
dependency and hamper students from coming to
grips with reality...

The inclination to indulge students may receive
further reinforcement from the teacher's fear
that any frustration will lead to an outburst of
unlimited anger. If the teacher himself is
inclined to react with violent rage to the
absence of gratification, it will make him so
frightened of his students' hostile attacks that
he may be unable to enforce limits.
(1983:50)

Basic psychoanalytic concepts, then, can be applied
to understanding the dynamics of the classroom. In
particular, notions such as the unconscious, the
predominance of childhood psychic life and
transference, can be used to make sense of the
'emotionality' of teaching and learning and the ways
in which this finds expression.

Individual identity and society

Freud's view of the relationship between person and
society needs to be understood in the context of his
description of the basic structures of personality.
Briefly, he distinguishes between three components
of personality: the id, ego and super-ego. Only the
id is present at birth. It is a reservoir of
instinctual energy. It has no direction, it is
illogical, unorganised, it is simply a mass of
excitation. It operates according to the primary
process, which discharges instinctual energy without
regard to reality. Its goal is twofold, to reduce
the excitation of the organism (the Nirvana
principle) and to increase affective pleasure and
decrease affective unpleasure or pain (the pleasure
principle). In attaining these goals, all it can do
is wish. This may result in short term tension
reduction, but ultimately the organism must take
reality into account if its wishes are to be
fulfilled.
    The development of the ego arises from this need
to perceive reality. The ego also pursues pleasure
and seeks to avoid unpleasure or pain. However, it
operates according to the reality principle: it
perceives, remembers, thinks and acts on the world.

It performs a mediating role between the demands of
the instinct and the action that will satisfy it.
The ego adapts to reality, and part of this reality
is social. Thus the ego must <u>understand</u> the moral
and ethical codes of society, its values, ideals and
taboos. Such an understanding is necessary for the
ego to appraise the consequences of a given course
of action. For example, violating a moral code in
the pursuit of pleasure will result in some form of
punishment by an external agent, usually the
parent. A crucial point for Freud is that in the
course of development, sanctions for wrong-doing
come to be administered internally via one's
conscience. Thus emerges the third component of
personality structure, the super-ego.

> Even if conscience is something 'within us' yet
> it is not so from the first. In this it is a
> real contrast to sexual life, which is in fact
> there from the beginning of life and not only a
> later addition. But, as is well known, young
> children are amoral and possess no internal
> inhibitions against their impulses striving for
> pleasure. The part which is later taken on by
> the super-ego is played to begin with by an
> external power, by parental authority ... It is
> only subsequently that the secondary situation
> develops where the external restraint is
> internalized and the super-ego takes the place
> of the parental agency and observes, directs and
> threatens the ego in exactly the same way as
> earlier the parents did with the child.
> (1973b:93)

The super-ego represents the claims of morality, it
is the internal means of judging good from bad.
Thoughts or actions which violate social
prescriptions are censured by the conscience and
feelings of guilt or shame are generated. In
contrast, thoughts or actions which approximate the
ego ideal (an idealised abstraction of parental or
social values) give rise to feelings of pride and
self-esteem.
   The above view of personality structure implies
that there is a necessary conflict between person
and society. This is because the basic instincts,
which derive from bodily needs, are essentially
anti-social. The person is caught in a dilemma.
Other people are necessary for instinctual
gratification but the co-operation of others is not
possible without ordered social life. Yet ordered

social life presupposes a degree of instinctual
renunciation (for example, the restriction of
aggressiveness). A unique insight of Freud was his
claim that the external conflict between person and
society becomes transformed into an internal
psychological conflict between the structures within
the personality. This is expressed in the following
passage from 'Civilization and its Discontents':

> Another question concerns us more nearly. What
> means does civilization employ in order to
> inhibit the aggressiveness which opposes it, to
> make it harmless, to get rid of it, perhaps? We
> have already become acquainted with a few of
> these methods, but not yet with the one that
> appears to be the most important. This we can
> study in the history of the development of the
> individual. What happens in him to render his
> desire for aggression innocuous? Something very
> remarkable, which we should never have guessed
> and which is nevertheless quite obvious. His
> aggressiveness is introjected, internalized; it
> is, in point of fact, sent back to where it came
> from - that is, it is directed towards his own
> ego. There it is taken over by a portion of the
> ego, which sets itself over against the rest of
> the ego as super-ego, and which now, in the form
> of 'conscience', is ready to put into action
> against the ego the same harsh aggressiveness
> that the ego would have liked to satisfy upon
> other, extraneous individuals. The tension
> between the harsh super-ego and the ego that is
> subjected to it, is called by us the sense of
> guilt; it expresses itself as a need for
> punishment. Civilization, therefore, obtains
> mastery over the individual's dangerous desire
> for aggression by weakening and disarming it and
> by setting up an agency within him to watch over
> it, like a garrison in a conquered city.
> (1963:60-1)

This explains a later remark by Freud that the price
we pay for civilisation is a heightened sense of
guilt. And it also places in perspective Fromm's
comment on the truly tragic picture of history that
Freud presents.

> Progress, beyond a certain point ... is in
> principle impossible. Man is only a battlefield
> on which the life and death instincts fight each
> other. He can never liberate himself decisively

> from the tragic alternative of destroying others
> or himself.   (1973:66)

Freud, it seems, set an upper limit on our capacity
for happiness and psychological health. This social
thrust within psychoanalysis was both developed and
challenged by subsequent work within the
psychoanalytic tradition. The politically radical
psychoanalytic thinkers such as Reich (1972) and
Marcuse (1969) reject the idea that instinctual
gratification and ordered social life are
incompatible. They regard repression (and its
associated concepts such as the Oedipus complex),
not as a necessary product of the human condition,
but as the product of a specific type of social
organisation, namely, the patriarchal authoritarian
one. For example, Reich claims that anti-social
impulses such as aggression are secondary, resulting
from the repression of natural biological needs. He
thus rejects the notion of anti-social instincts.

> Moral regulation represses and keeps from
> gratification the natural biological needs.
> This results in secondary pathological
> anti-social impulses. These in turn have to be
> inhibited of necessity. Thus, morality does not
> owe its existence to the necessity of inhibiting
> anti-social tendencies.   (1972:22)

In <u>Eros and Civilisation,</u> Marcuse points out that
Freud failed to distinguish between the level of
repression required to maintain society as such, and
the level required to support an oppressive social
structure. Both Reich and Marcuse tapped the
critical force of psychoanalysis and recognised its
potential as a basis for a theory of oppression – as
did others much later (e.g. the women's movement and
marxist intellectuals). Connell (1983) explores
this theme in his essay '<u>Dr Freud and the course of
history</u>', where he draws an analogy between the
psychoanalytic technique of 'decoding' the meanings
of unconscious material produced by patients (e.g.
dreams and symptoms) and the marxist analysis of
ideology. In the latter, many commonsense, everyday
understandings of life are 'decoded' or 'unmasked'
as distortions which serve to conceal domination and
exploitation.
     Thus the idea that we internalise the social
values of our parents and other authority figures,
gives us a glimpse of the way in which the social
structure is united to constraints that operate in

our personality. It assists us in explaining how we
can act against our own best interests and how
political, racial, class and sexual oppression can
become a constituent part of personality structure
and the conflicts within it. Connell offers the
following assessment:

> It is a psychology of impossible situations,
> where irresistible forces of lust and rage meet
> immovable obstacles of social relations and
> culture, and produce our lives as a result. It
> is a theory, in fact the only theory, that
> begins to account for the way oppressive
> situations are lived by the people in them, the
> way consciousness itself is distorted by
> psychological force majeure.   (1983:15)

Freud's characterisation of the relationship between
person and society is crucially important. The link
between social oppression and psychological
repression has occupied the attention of adult
educators working with oppressed groups (e.g.
Freire, 1972; Thompson, 1983). Psychoanalysis
offers us a theory which explains why some members
of oppressed groups fail to recognise their
oppression and may angrily denounce those who
attempt to convince them otherwise (organisations
like 'Women Who Want to be Women' provide a
collective outlet for such a denunciation). A key
issue for adult educators working with oppressed
groups is how best to conceive their role. One
approach is to consider adult education as a kind of
therapeutic exercise which offers relief from the
symptoms of repression/oppression by, say,
'assisting with personal growth' or 'building
confidence'. Keddie has criticised the conservatism
of this approach:

> Confidence for what or in what? Is adult
> education, through providing a 'women's
> interest' curriculum, enabling women to become
> more satisfied consumers of their own
> oppression? Is it making them more confident
> and competent managers of their homes, more able
> to cope with its tensions through courses in
> Yoga, slimmer and more attractive through Keep
> Fit and Beauty Culture, and meeting their needs
> for self-expression through classes in painting
> or creative writing? Does providing women with
> an interest outside the home and a creche for
> classes, give them a break from the children
> which makes them happier mothers and create more

> lively and informed wives who can show more
> interest in their husbands' work?   (cited in
> Thompson, 1983:84)

The alternative is for the adult educator to become
actively engaged in social change. Initially this
may be done by creating among learners a critical
awareness of the oppressive nature of their
position. A commitment to this approach brings with
it the issue of how the adult educator can best
assist in this process - an issue which will be
addressed in a later chapter. All this seems rather
remote from psychoanalysis, but it is worth
emphasising that psychological repression can be
interpreted as a response to forms of social
oppression.

Erikson's 'psychosocial' stages:
a psychoanalytic approach to adult development

Erikson describes personality growth in terms of a
sequence of stages which he labels 'psychosocial
stages'. As development proceeds, the ego alters to
meet the changing demands of society. This need to
adjust to society's demands promotes an emotional
crisis or conflict within the person. Erikson
identifies eight basic crises across the lifespan,
each one corresponding to a stage of development as
outlined in Table 3.1.

Table 3.1
Erikson's stages of psychosocial development

Psychosocial Stage	Characteristic Emotional Crisis
Oral - sensory	basic trust vs mistrust
Anal - musculature	autonomy vs shame, doubt
Genital - locomotor	initiative vs guilt
Latency	industry vs inferiority
Puberty and adolescence	identity vs role confusion
Young adulthood	intimacy vs isolation
Adulthood	generativity vs stagnation
Maturity	ego integrity vs despair

Erikson's earlier stages complement the psychosexual
stages of Freud. For example, he regards the oral -
sensory stage as being one where the child 'lives
through and lives with, his mouth .... To him the

36

mouth is the focus of a general first approach to
life - the incorporative approach.' (1959:57). At
this stage, the child's ego must be capable of
dealing with the wealth of sensory experiences it
encounters. If these experiences are basically
pleasant, the child will feel the world is benign
and supportive   - it will develop a sense of basic
trust. If the sensory experiences result in pain
and discomfort and the world appears to be a place
of pain and danger - then a sense of mistrust will
develop. The remaining childhood stages of
development also have close parallels with Freud's
psychosexual stages.   During the anal - musculature
stage the principal crisis centres on the child's
capacity to control its bodily movements and thereby
develop a sense of autonomy. Shame and doubt will
result from lack of control (e.g. of bowel
movements), shame because of others' disapproval,
and doubt because of one's feeling of incompetence.
The genital stage has close links with Freud's
phallic stage   - the child, in resolving its Oedipal
conflict (i.e. the conflict between rivalry and
identification with the same sex) is drawn into a
general crisis of initiative (which is an expression
of independence from parental ties) versus guilt
(where a continued dependence on parents is in
conflict with society's expectations). The latency
stage is a time when children are expected to
acquire the basic skills which prepare them for
adult life - in western society this takes the form
of schooling. The sense of industry or inferiority
is predicated on the child's capacity to acquire
these skills. Finally, the stage of puberty and
adolescence corresponds to the genital stage in
Freudian theory. Unlike Freud, who is primarily
concerned with the emergence of a genital sex drive,
Erikson is concerned with the implications of all
the changes which occur during adolescence (i.e.
physiological and physical changes together with the
changing expectations of society). These changes
result in an identity crisis for adolescents. They
are confronted with the task of defining themselves
and making a commitment to their social roles;
failure to do so results in identity confusion. At
this point, the parallels with Freudian psychosexual
stages cease and Erikson describes a further three
stages of adult development. The first adult stage,
young adulthood, centres on the crisis of intimacy.
Will the developing person have the capacity to form
intimate relationships with others or will he or she
become self-absorbed? The answer depends largely on

the outcome of earlier crises, in particular, the
identity crisis of adolescence.

> But it is only after a reasonable sense of
> identity has been established that real intimacy
> with the other sex (or, for that matter, with
> any other person or even with oneself) is
> possible. ....the condition of a true twoness is
> that one must first become oneself.   (1959:95)

The next stage, adulthood, focuses on whether the
person has a sense of being a productive,
contributing member of society (generativity) or
whether they feel unable to contribute
(stagnation). In the final stage, integrity is the
culmination of the successful resolution of life's
developmental crises. 'It is the acceptance of
one's own and only life cycle ... it is a sense of
comradeship with men and women of distant times and
of different pursuits.' (1959:98). Opposed to
integrity is the sense of despair which is
characterised by a fear of death and a failure to
accept one's personal history.
    Even though Erikson emphasises changing social
demands as being the catalyst for individual growth
and development, he does not dispense with the
(psychoanalytic) view that maturation plays a
central role. He maintains that the human organism
has a 'ground plan' which obeys 'inner laws of
development'.

> Personality can be said to develop according to
> steps predetermined in the human organism's
> readiness to be driven forward, to be aware of,
> and to interact with a widening social
> radius.   (1959:52)

Thus personality development is governed by a
maturational timetable. This means that the
development of capabilities like trust, autonomy,
initiative and industry, only occur during critical
periods of life. If these capabilities do not
emerge when they are supposed to, then their optimum
development will be impaired and subsequent
development will be unfavourably affected. That is,
intimacy is predicated on identity, identity upon
industry and industry upon initiative, etc.
    To sum up, the psychosocial stages occur in an
invariant sequence, and the resolution of each
successive crisis leaves an indelible impression on
personality, which moreover influences the

resolution of subsequent crises.

The outcome of the successful resolution of life's developmental crises is the healthy integrated personality. The healthy personality charters a course through each crisis 'emerging and re-emerging with an increased sense of inner unity, with an increase of good judgement and an increase in the capacity to do well, according to the standards of those who are significant to him' (1959:51).

Erikson's theory broadens and extends the Freudian psychosexual stages through a focus on the emergence of identity and a stress on the impact of social demands. Similarly, his concept of the healthy personality is cast more positively than Freud's, instead of being a compromise between instinctual gratification and the demands of social life, the healthy personality emerges from the positive resolution of a series of emotional crises. Nevertheless, Erikson's theory is firmly entrenched in the psychoanalytic tradition, testimony to this is the use of psychoanalytic concepts and the importance attached to maturation and the experiences of childhood. Like Freud, he postulates a structure of ego development which is universal – it is only the psychological content of the crisis resolutions which are cultural and historical. In this sense, his theory is as rigid as Freud's.

The most important critique of Erikson (Jacoby, 1975; Roazen, 1976) is that his theory is conformist and supports the status quo. Even though he expresses an awareness of alienating and repressive social forces, his view of psychological health is couched in terms of how well the person adapts to society's needs. Thus Buss remarks:

> I can imagine a society where the more valid reaction is shame and doubt rather than autonomy, guilt rather than initiative, identity diffusion rather than identity. The conflict and confusions that an individual experiences may represent a healthy response to a social reality that is psychologically (not to mention physically) repressive, alienating and constricting. Integration of the individual into society is not an absolute to be unquestioningly sought after. (1979:328)

Ironically, while Erikson seeks to avoid the ahistorical nature of orthodox psychoanalysis, the alternative he offers is an ahistorical view of the healthy personality as one which adapts to the demands of a particular social/historical world. In rejecting Freud's pessimistic view, which allows little scope for progress in the human condition, Erikson portrays the person-society relationship as one characterised by harmony - and the development of a healthy personality is predicated on this harmony.

To sum up, both Erikson and Freud have much to say about the relationship between individual psychology and social organisation, but neither develop a social critique. Freud considers internal psychological conflict to be a necessary product of civilisation - <u>any</u> civilisation - thus mental health and happiness is limited by civilisation per se. Erikson sees mental health as attainable but defines it in terms of how people successfully adjust to the demands of society. The possibility that some forms of social organisation are alienating and psychologically unhealthy, while others are liberating and psychologically healthy, was not systematically explored by them. This theme was elaborated by later more radical psychoanalytic thinkers who latched on to the social thrust of psychoanalysis - a thrust which is still being developed and which is apparent, at least implicitly, in the thinking of some adult educators.

Chapter Four

ADULT DEVELOPMENT

Adult educators, who in many respects are critical consumers of ideas about teaching and learning, seem to have a weakness when it comes to critically evaluating theory and research in adult development. This weakness is perhaps due to the belief that the identity of adult education is premised on the identity of the adult. Hence the literature on adult development is attractive because it offers (however illusory the offer may be) the promise of a distinct and coherent theory of adult learning.

Published accounts of the adult learning process nearly always make reference to lifespan developmental stages, the life cycle or the 'phases' of adult life. In a similar way many policy documents in adult and continuing education stress the importance of addressing the needs associated with adult development and growth. Allman (1982) sets out the case for this interest in adult development. She observes that studies of adult life reveal it to be a period of change and development, much like that of childhood and adolescence. She argues that the results of such studies serve notice on the prevailing assumptions about adulthood – that it is a long period of stability where previously learned capacities, skills, attitudes and values are applied to one's activities at work, in the family, in leisure and in civic life. These assumptions need to be challenged because they 'clearly affect decision makers in the field of politics, education and social policy' (1982: 42). In education they are linked to the conventional view that the period of initial education equips young adults for the remainder of their working lives – a view which continues to inform political debate on educational priorities.

There is also a need, according to Allman, to disseminate knowledge about adult development to the community at large: 'It is also urgent that these ideas begin to permeate the realm of common sense, as all adults are continually in the process of making personal life decisions which may be based on similar highly questionable assumptions about their own potential for growth and development' (1982: 43). Arguments like these are convincing and we do need to revise our outmoded views about adult life. But, as I shall argue, we need to proceed with caution, otherwise there is a risk of replacing one set of false beliefs with another equally false (albeit more palatable) set of beliefs about adult development.

The first part of this chapter reviews some of the connections which have been made between adult development and adult education. The second part focuses on evaluating the adequacy of existing theory and research in this area.

A question commonly posed by those with an interest in adult learning is: 'What are the implications of adult development for adult and continuing education practitioners?' Knox (1979) outlines three possible implications:

1. To predict and explain success in education: 'Practitioners are typically interested in developmental generalizations regarding performance or personality in order to predict and explain successful participation in educative activity' (1979:59).
2. To help people adapt to changing adult roles: 'Adult life cycle trends in performance in family, occupational and community roles suggest ways in which continuing education participation might facilitate adaptation and growth related to each role area' (1979:59).
3. To improve the effectiveness of marketing and instructional activities: 'From time to time, the stability of adulthood is punctuated by role change events such as the birth of the first child, a move to another community or retirement ... Such change events typically produce heightened readiness to learn which, if recognized, can contribute to the effectiveness of marketing and instructional activities' (1979:60).

The whole tenor of the above implications indicates a view about adult development and an attitude to

42

adult education. That is, that the various 'roles' of adult life are inevitable and people must learn to cope with them as they arise; and that adult education agencies, if they wish to be successful, should gear their marketing and instructional activities to cater for the different needs of adults at different life stages. There is no sense in which adult roles are portrayed as arbitrary or even oppressive, or that alternative roles and options are possible for a given life period. In this sense adult education contributes towards the maintenance of social norms and structures. One need not look very far to find other instances of this type of approach. A significant example can be found in McCoy's (1977) tabulation of 'Adult Life Cycle Tasks and Educational Program Responses' which is reproduced in Chickering's (1981) influential volume 'The Modern American College'. McCoy identifies seven developmental stages, each of which is characterised by a set of common tasks. For example, the 'leaving home' stage (18-22) has the associated tasks of 'break psychological ties', 'choose career', 'enter work', 'manage time' and so on. Each stage is then related to an appropriate range of program responses, with a final column indicating the outcomes sought from the educational program. The table is too lengthy to reproduce here but a cross-section of one stage only will be sufficient to illustrate the general strategy. Table 4.1 shows the 'tasks' and 'program responses' appropriate for the developmental stage 'Becoming adult'.

A casual glance at the list of tasks and how each of them relates to specified programs confirms my general point about adult education supporting the status quo. Even a non-specific 'task' such as 'achieving autonomy', is interpreted in the most narrow sense possible, that is, as the capacity to 'live alone successfully'. It is unnecessary to elaborate further, the tabulation speaks for itself. What is surprising, and disappointing, is that anyone in adult education would take such an analysis seriously as anything other than a narrow descriptive exercise.

Yet there is a strongly held view among adult educators that the everyday reality of learners should be acknowledged, no matter how culturally specific that reality may be. The reader may remonstrate that McCoy is simply following this precept - what, then, is so objectionable? As I see it, there are two objections. The first of these is

Table 4.1: Educational responses to life cycle tasks

Task	Program responses
1. Select mate	Marriage workshops
2. Settle in work, begin career ladder	Management, advancement training
3. Parent	Parenting workshops
4. Become involved in community	Civic education; volunteer training
5. Consume wisely	Consumer education; financial management training
6. Home-own	Home-owning, maintenance workshops
7. Socially interact	Human relations groups, TA
8. Achieve autonomy	Living alone, divorce workshops
9. Problem-solve	Creative problem-solving workshops
10. Manage stress accompanying change	Stress management, biofeedback, relaxation, TM workshops

Source: McCoy (1977)

that there is no acknowledgement of the narrow culturally specific 'tasks' which are identified. Quite the opposite, the 'tasks' are presented as a generalisable framework to be used by adult education agencies in formulating their programs. There is no sense in which McCoy is using her analysis as a case study of a process for others to emulate in a different cultural context. The second objection, already mentioned in relation to Knox, is that the response of adult education is depicted as solely adaptive. There is no scope for questioning and challanging the tasks - they constitute the taken for granted reality of the learners _and_ the adult educators.

There are many adult educators who, being dismissive of the above approach, nevertheless subscribe to the view that adult development is a central concept in adult education. An interest in adult development stems quite naturally from a commitment to the notion of lifelong learning and the associated concepts of 'lifelong education', 'recurrent education' and 'education permanent'. The policy and research documents of UNESCO, the OECD and the Council of Europe, which are the major sponsoring bodies of these concepts, frequently cite adult development as a central concern of any lifelong learning strategy. However, they do not understand adult development to be an immutable sequence of stages through which people pass at more or less predictable ages. Indeed, they challenge the concept of the 'typical' life cycle and support their view with an analysis of contemporary social and economic change. This is particularly apparent in the literature on recurrent education, and the following extract, taken from an article by one of its chief proponents, Jarl Bengtsson, typifies this approach:

> ... significant changes are taking place in the relationship between work and non-work time seen over the individual's whole life cycle in terms of increased education, earlier retirement, longer holidays, etc. It has also been made clear that these changes affect social groups according to their hierarchical position in working life, as well as the way their work is being scheduled, i.e. full-time, part-time, shiftwork, long spells of employment, etc.

> The claim is not that more non-work time is or will be used for education, although that certainly remains a strong possibility. Rather it is that to look at recurrent education from this perspective provides a very useful point of departure for placing it in the broader context of emerging new life-styles and life cycles. Most likely, the crucial factors behind changes in the individual's lifecycle pattern will be the economic and employment conditions that the industrialized countries will face during coming years.   (1979:26)

Recurrent education, and its closely related concepts, accepts the diversity of life cycle patterns and the need for educational institutions

to respond to and foster this diversity through a
diversity of provision. It supports the notion that
individual options should be extended, especially
the way in which paid work, unpaid work, education
and leisure are combined. The principles espoused
can be seen as a response to the effects of social,
economic and technological change. Changes in
demographic patterns, the sexual division of labour,
the length of working life, hours spent at work,
retirement age and so on, are all seen as relevant
to the proposition that educational opportunities
should be distributed, in a recurring way, across
the lifespan. Recurrent education also embodies the
notion of social justice and its evolution as a
concept from the late 1960s has been linked with a
host of terms implying broad social reforms:
industrial democracy, participation in planning,
social equity, decentralisation, links between
education and work and between younger and older
generations, and concern with the disadvantaged. An
underlying value in all this is a humanistic concern
for the individual. The idea of self-development,
which is based on notions of individuality and
growth, is contrasted with the opposing notions of
enslavement, alienation and stagnation – which are
the psychological consequences of clinging to an
outmoded conception of the 'normal' life cycle.
    Research and theory in adult development is not
always concerned with identifying so called 'normal'
life patterns. A bevy of theoretical perspectives
and research techniques have been deployed to make
sense of the experience of adulthood. The resulting
literature is diverse and difficult to harnass,
especially for adult educators who often want only
to apply a few general (and unambiguous) principles
to their practice. Generally speaking, however, the
narrowly focused, neatly presented and least
ambiguous 'principles' are those which are the most
questionable. This theme will now be expanded and
illustrated more thoroughly in the remainder of this
chapter.
    There are two persistent problems which are a
feature of adult developmental psychology. The
first is that there are insurmountable
methodological difficulties in establishing 'phases'
or 'stages' of adult life. The second is that much
of the literature is historically and socially
rooted and lacks any worthwhile generalisability.

Methodological difficulties

I have dealt elsewhere in the text with some of the
conceptual and methodological problems in
stage-development research. Not all adult
development studies adopt a stage-sequence approach,
nevertheless, they usually have a stake in making
comparisons between different 'ages', 'phases' or
'stages' of life. Leaving aside the problem of
deciding what type of data to gather, the common
methodological problem is to construct a research
design which generates comparative data (on whatever
dimension) which indicates the effects of age
changes only (where the effects of other factors,
such as 'history' and 'time of measurement' are
neutralised). Many of the most influential studies
in adult development use research designs which fail
to do this. Three basic research designs are the
'cross-sectional', 'longitudinal' and 'time - lag'
designs. These are illustrated in Figure 4.1.

Figure 4.1
Adult development: basic research designs

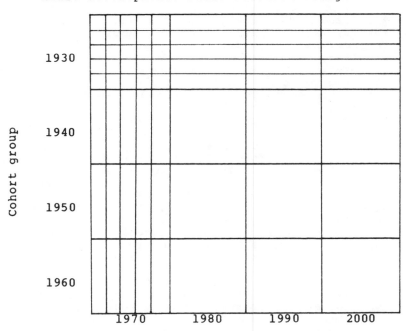

Time of measurement

The cross-sectional design is represented by each of the columns. It is where two or more age cohorts are investigated at <u>one</u> time of measurement. The hypothetical example in the table appears in the left hand column, where at one time of measurement (1970) data are gathered from four age cohorts (people born in 1930, 1940, 1950, 1960). Perhaps the best known example of this technique is to be found in the research of Gould (1972). In an initial study Gould (1972) observed and recorded the concerns expressed by a number of psychiatric outpatients. He hypothesised that these concerns differed among different age groups. He then used these expressed concerns to construct a questionnaire which contained 160 questions divided into ten areas of life. This questionnaire was then administered, in a later study, to a sample of 524 non-patients, who were white middle class men and women aged 16-50 years. They were required to rank a selection of statements according to their personal applicability, as shown in Table 4.2.

The difficulty with a research design such as this is that the observed differences in 'concerns' may be due to the different life experiences of the different age cohorts. For example, the life history of a 50-year-old in 1972 would necessarily include the 'great depression' of the 1930s and the experience of World War II. This would be quite different from the life history of a 22-year-old in 1972 who would have experienced (as a child and youth) the economic boom of the post-WWII years and the social changes of the 1960s. It seems reasonable to assume that such historical events and trends affect peoples' 'concerns'. Indeed they may be more significant in explaining the different concerns of different age cohorts than any hypothesised notion of the life cycle.

One way to avoid making comparisons between different cohorts is to investigate a single age cohort over a number of years. This is referred to as a longitudinal design and is represented by the rows in Figure 4.1. The horizontal lines on the top row provide a hypothetical example. A sample of people born in 1930 could be studied at different times, in 1970 (40 years), 1980 (50 years), 1990 (60 years) and 2000 (70 years). The Grant Study (Vaillant, 1977) provides a good example of this type of research design. Ninety-four college graduates from the early 1940s were followed through until 1969. They were part of an initial study of 268 male undergraduates who were given extensive

Table 4.2
A sample of statements from Gould's questionnaire

1. I feel that some exciting things are going to happen to me.
2. I never plan on what tomorrow may bring.
3. It hurts me to realise that I will not get some things in life I want.
4. I live for today, forget the past.
5. I think things aren't as good as they used to be.
6. I believe I will some day have everything I want in life.
7. My life doesn't change much from year to year.
8. There is little hope for the future.
9. I try to be satisfied with what I have and not to think so much about the things I probably won't be able to get.
10. I wish I could change the past.
11. I dream about life ten years from now.
12. I spend more time now thinking about the past than about the future.
13. There's still plenty of time to do most of the things I want to do.
14. I would be quite content to remain as old as I am now.
15. I find myself daydreaming about good experiences in the past.
16. I will have to settle for less than I expected, but I still think I will get most things I want.

Source: Gould, 1972:39

physiological and psychological examinations early in their college years. After graduation the sample of 94 graduates completed annual questonnaires until 1955, and every two years after that date. They were interviewed in their homes twice, in 1950-52 and in 1969. Vaillant (1977) reports the results in detail, but his thesis is simple: that ego defence mechanisms mature through the life cycle and that healthy adults progress through a hierarchy of adaptive mechanisms as shown in Table 4.3.

There are some well documented problems with longitudinal studies, such as experimental mortality (where participants drop out of the study) and practice effects (where the participants become overly familiar with the style of the questionnaire and the structure of the interview) and time-of-measurement effects (where measurements, because they are taken at different times, may only

Table 4.3: Hierarchy of adaptive mechanisms

Level I: Psychotic mechanisms (common in
            psychosis, dreams, childhood)

Denial (of external reality)
Distortion
Delusional projection

Level II: Immature mechanisms (common in severe
            depression, personality disorders and
            adolescence)

Fantasy (schizoid withdrawal, denial through fantasy)
Projection
Hypochondriasis
Passive-aggressive behaviour (masochism, turning
against the self)
Acting out (compulsive delinquency, perversion)

Level III: Neurotic mechanisms (common in everyone)

Intellectualization (isolation, obsessive behaviour,
undoing, rationalization)
Repression
Reaction formation
Displacement (conversion, phobias, wit)
Dissociation (neurotic denial)

Level IV: Mature mechanisms (common in 'healthy'
            adults)

Sublimation
Altruism
Suppression
Anticipation
Humor

Source: Vaillant, 1977:80

reflect changed social and cultural conditions). A
significant problem, and one often overlooked is
that over, say, a thirty year period, there are
bound to be shifts in the theoretical perspective of
the theory upon which the research is based. This
often means that the initial questions and modes of
analysis become obsolescent and are replaced by more

contemporary techniques. This certainly happened in
Vaillant's study:

> Unfortunately, the work of four other innovative
> students of personality in the 1930s was
> ignored. I say unfortunately because the work
> of these four men and women has affected my
> interpretation of the results of the Study.
> Erik Erikson, Anna Freud, Harry Stack Sullivan
> and Heinz Hartmann all significantly influenced
> modern understanding of personality; but in
> 1937-1942 their work was still too novel to
> shape the early design of the Grant Study.
>
> By 1940 Harry Stack Sullivan had begun to
> revolutionize the psychodynamic theory of
> personality. Slowly, Sullivan and his British
> counterpart, Melanie Klein, led psychiatrists to
> realize that interpersonal relations played as
> important a role in shaping personality as did
> the intrapersonal relations between ego,
> conscience and instinct, but not before the
> Grant Study was well under way. For example,
> although in college the psychiatric interviews
> had included a careful history of adolescent
> sexual development, the Study psychiatrists did
> not inquire into the boys' friendship patterns,
> or their efforts at heterosexual intimacy. Not
> until 1950, really, did the Grant Study begin to
> pay close attention to the men's relationships
> with older men and women.
>
> In 1937 Anna Freud first published in English
> 'The Ego and The Mechanisms of Defense' and
> Heinz Hartmann had presented in German 'Ego
> Psychology and the Problem of Adaptation'. Not
> until 1967 did the Grant Study focus on these
> men's styles of psychological adaptation.
>
> In the late 1930s at the University of
> California Erikson had begun the work that in
> 1950 was to culminate in 'Childhood and Society'
> - providing convincing evidence that adults
> mature as well as children. During the same
> period, the Grant Study staff, like their
> colleagues elsewhere, saw psychodynamic
> maturation as being largely completed by
> adolescence. (1977:43-4).

Even though longitudinal studies overcome the
problems of comparing different cohorts, they

nevertheless remain historically bound. This means
that generalisations to different cohort groups can
only be made on the assumption that historical
variation is unimportant.

Is it possible to avoid the influence of
historical variation? The answer to this question
rests heavily on one's analysis of how history and
culture influence the psychological make-up of
individuals. From a research design point of view
it is certainly possible to control for historical
effects by using some combination of longitudinal
and cross-sectional designs. For example, combining
the first two vertical columns in Figure 4.1 would
represent a cross-sectional sequence where all four
cohort groups are investigated twice, once in 1970
and again in 1980. Similarly, combining the bottom
two rows would represent a longitudinal sequence,
where two cohort groups are investigated
simultaneously over a number of years (1970-2000).
Through such techniques it is possible to obtain
data about the effects of cohort differences,
time-of-measurement differences and age
differences. For example, the differences between
20-year-olds (1970-80) can be compared with the
differences between 30-year-olds (1980-90) in order
to gauge the effect of cohort membership on the
general difference between 20 and 30 year olds.
This, in effect, is a way of 'controlling' for
historical variation. But the control gained
through such a practice is very limited. Firstly,
it depends on whether the changes being monitored
are easily quantifiable. In fact, most of the
studies of this kind have been developed by those
with an interest in measuring the development of
human abilities, especially intellectual development
(eg. Schaie, 1979). The research designs employed
were initially intended to partial out the
historical effects of improvements in educational
provision during (longitudinal) or between
(cross-sectional) the lifetimes of the subjects
being studied. This is easy to do when it is simply
a matter of comparing test scores, but it is a
dubious task to make such comparisons with
qualitative data of the kind found in adult
personality development. Secondly, there is an
assumption that the impact of history is linear and
cumulative. But this is an untenable assumption (eg.
a 20-year-old in 1975 may be quite different from a
20-year-old in 1970 or 1980).

Another way of minimising the impact of
historical variation on developmental research is to

gather 'data' of a high level of generality.
Gould's questionnaire addressed those sorts of
things which are historically and socially specific
(views about marriage, career, children, etc).
However, other investigators have pitched their
analysis at a more general level. For example,
Lowenthal et al (1977) used a cross-sectional
technique to investigate the adaptive processes of
men and women across the lifespan. In their study
they documented such general psychological qualities
as complexity, self image, expressiveness and
perceptions in continuity of value structure. The
biographical interview technique of Levinson (1978)
was primarily aimed at elucidating changes in the
relationship between self and world throughout the
life course. Loevinger (1976) was also concerned
with the rather abstract notion of ego as a central
frame of reference for understanding self and
others. However, a closer look at this research
will still reveal its social and historical
specificity.

Social and historical bias

In the immediately preceding section on
methodological difficulties I outlined some of the
research design problems when comparing different
people of different ages at a given time
(cross-sectional) or when comparing the same people
at different ages (longitudinal). I argued that
historical events either confound the results of any
comparison or they limit the generalisability of the
results.
     There is another, less direct way in which
'history' can affect research in adult development.
Research is necessarily conducted in a particular
social and historical context, but good research
should produce results which are generalisable
beyond that context. Unfortunately, research in
adult development, especially the genre concerned
with life 'stages' or 'phases', seems prone to
social and historical bias. This is evident in four
ways; the existence of purely descriptive
inventories of life 'tasks', the selection of
subjects for research, the data gathering
techniques, and the way in which the concept of the
'healthy' personality is constructed.

Descriptive inventories
Reference has already been made to McCoy's (1977)
tabulation 'Adult Life Cycle Tasks and Educational

Program Responses'. This approach, whereby an inventory of life tasks is constructed, has its origins in Havighurst's (1972) 'Developmental Tasks and Education' which was written in the early 1940s. Table 4.4 is a modified version of Havighurst's original set of developmental tasks. It is similar to the inventory of McCoy (1977) and the same objections apply here. It is worthwhile noting, however, Havighurst's comments on his original inventory.

> The tasks the individual must learn - the developmental tasks of life - are those things that constitute healthy and satisfactory growth in our society. They are the things a person must learn if he is to be judged and to judge himself to be a reasonably happy and successful person. A developmental task is a task which arises at or about a certain period in the life of the individual, successful achievement of which leads to his happiness and to success with later tasks, while failure leads to unhappiness in the individual, disapproval by the society, and difficulty with later tasks.   (1972:2)

Thus the developmental tasks of life amount to a socially approved timetable for individual growth and development. In a pluralistic society this timetable will differ between social groups. While it may be useful to identify the developmental tasks of particular social or community groups, as Tucker and Huerta (1987) have done in their study of Mexican-American females, it is dangerous to generalise about the developmental tasks of society as such.

Sample selection, data gathering techniques
Table 4.5 sets out the sample, method and developmental processes identified by each of six well known adult developmental psychologists. Five of these gathered data prior to formulating their views about adult development. An impressionistic description of the samples used is that they consisted of North American, white, middle class, better educated, predominantly male subjects.
      The techniques for gathering data were the structured interview, questionnaire, self rating checklist, standard psychological test and observer rating. But one should be wary of accepting reported results without a detailed knowledge of how these techniques were applied in each case. For

Table 4.4:   Developmental tasks of the adult years

16-23 Late Adolescence and Youth	23-35 Early Adulthood	35-45 Midlife Transition	45-57 Middle Adulthood	57-65 Late Adult Transition	65+ Late Adulthood
Achieving emotional independence					
Preparing for marriage and family life					
Choosing and preparing for a career					
Developing an ethical system					
	Deciding on a partner				
	Starting a family				
	Managing a home				
	Starting in an occupation				
	Assuming civic responsibilities				
		Adapting to a changing time perspective			
		Revising career plans			
		Redefining family relationships			
			Maintaining a career or developing a new one		
			Restabilizing family relationships		
			Making mature civic contributions		
			Adjusting to biological change		
				Preparing for retirement	
					Adjusting to retirement
					Adjusting to declining health and strength
					Becoming affiliated with late-adult age groups
					Establishing satisfactory living arrangements
					Adjusting to the death of a spouse
					Maintaining integrity

Source: Chickering and Havighurst (1981)

Table 4.5: Some methods and views on the developmental process

Theorist	Sample	Method	Developmental process
Levinson (1978) The life cycle of men	. Forty men, 35-45 years old in 1968-70. All American born. 10 biologists, 10 blue collar workers, 10 novelists, 10 business executives. . Social class: varied. . Race, ethnicity: mixture. . Education: 70% completed college. . Marital status: all had been married at least once.	. Biographical interviewing 10-20 hours each. . Test as part of interview. Task was to construct the 'story' of each man's life. . Interview protocols provided basis for generalisations about the life cycle.	. Building and modifying life structures (basic pattern of a person's life). Alternation of stable and transitional periods in life structure. . Individualisation proceeds throughout the course of life - this refers to the relationship between self and the external world.
Gould (1979) Stages in the development of adult consciousness	. 125 psychiatric residents . unspecified number of psychiatric out-patients . non-patients, 524, 16-50 years, white and middle class men and women.	. Cross-sectional. . Questionnaire and therapeutic observations. . Questionnaire contained statements based on expressed concerns of psychiatric patients: 160 questions on 10 areas of life - each area requiring a forced ranking of statements according to personal applicability (self-rating).	. People strive for a fuller more independent adult consciousness. . Growth implies reformulating our self definition and overcoming childhood consciousness. . Growth implies shedding the unconscious and restrictive set of protective devices which form the safety boundary of childhood ie. overcoming major false assumptions.
Lowenthal (1977) Four stages of life	. 216 urban men and women, largely Caucasian, middle and lower-middle class. . Four groups: High School mean age 17 Newlywed " " 24 Middle aged " " 50 Pre-retirement " " 60	. Cross-sectional. . Interviews (8 hours): - structural interview schedule and - measures and rating related to adaptation.	. No global theoretical framework - but uses a range of theoretical concepts to understand adaptive processes across the lifespan eg. complexity, expressiveness, self-image, life satisfaction, perspectives on past and future, perceived stress, perceptions of continuity in value structure.

Chickering & Havighurst (1981) Adult developmental tasks	No direct research reported.	Relies on a range of developmental phase studies.	Three sources of developmental tasks: 1. physical/biological 2. social/cultural life 3. personal values and aspirations of the individual
Loevinger (1976) Ego development	A number of studies using undergraduate students.	• Systematic comparison of her stages with those of other stage theorists eg Erikson, Fromm, Piaget, Sullivan, Kohlberg, Perry. • Projective tests requiring sentence completion (eg education is ...)	• Ego is a central frame of reference for understanding self and others. • There is a developmental movement from simple stereotyped thinking and perceptions to a more complex and differentiated view of self and world.
Vaillant (1977) Heirarchy of adaptive mechanisms	Initially 268 male under-graduates (39-44). 94 male graduates followed up in 1969 - average age 47.	Longitudinal (Grant Study) interviews and annual questionnaires. Initially extensive physical, physiological and psychological examinations.	• Ego defence mechanisms mature through the life cycle - especially for those who were psychosocially mature in Erikson's sense.

example, in reporting the results of his longitudinal study of men Vaillant (1977) at one point describes the association between psychological maturity and external adjustment. In Table 4.6 he compares the men with the 'best life outcomes' and 'worst life outcomes' (determined by an independent adjustment scale) on the dimension of psychological maturity. He compares them on the basis of how they fare on a number of 'external adjustment' indicators which include 'failure to marry by 30', 'children admitted to father's college' and 'average yearly charitable contribution'. True, the bulk of Vaillant's work is rich in detail and full of insights into the psychological dynamics of the participants, but this one table is sufficient to make the reader hesitant to accept his thesis in other respects. This is because it reveals a rating technique which employs highly questionable indicators.

Table 4.6
Differences between best and worst outcomes
relevant to an Eriksonian model of the life cycle

	Best Outcomes (30 men)	Worst Outcomes (30 men)
Childhood environment poor	17%	47%
Pessimism, self-doubt, passivity and fear of sex at 50	3%	50%
In college personality integration put in bottom fifth	0	33%
Subjects whose career choice reflected identification with father	60%	27%
Dominated by mother in adult life	0	40%
Failure to marry by 30	3%	37%
Bleak friendship patterns by 50	0	57%
Current job has little supervisory responsibility	20%	93%
Children admitted to father's college	47%	10%
Children's outcome described as good or excellent	66%	23%
Average yearly charitable contribution	$3,000	$500

Source: Vaillant, 1977:350

Conceptions of the healthy personality

Development implies growth and progress, not merely change. But growth and progress towards what end? The answer to this question is often the starting point for theories of adult development, and it is the conception of the end point of development, the 'mature' or 'healthy' personality which frequently governs how progress and growth is monitored and explained within a given theory. For Kohlberg, growth is towards autonomous and principled morality, for Erikson, towards inner unity, and for Maslow, it is towards self-actualisation with its increased sense of self and autonomy. Many developmental psychologists construe the end point of development with terms like 'individuality', 'autonomy' and the 'integrated self'.

But do such descriptions represent a particular way of looking at the world which excludes certain cultures or sections of the population? A closer look may help to resolve this issue. Levinson, for example, makes the following remarks about the 'individuation' process.

> Throughout the life cycle, but especially in the key transition periods such as infancy, pubescence and the Mid-life Transition, the developmental process of individuation is going on. This term refers to the changes in a person's relationship to himself and to the external world. The infant, leaving his mother's womb, must gain some idea of his separate existence. He must decide where he stops and where the world begins. He must separate himself from his mother, yet maintain a tie to her. He must form a sense of 'reality' that allows him to accept his surroundings as having an independent existence not necessarily subject to his control. The child's world gradually expands to include his family, neighborhood and friends; and his self becomes more complex through his relationships with other persons and institutions.

> These changes are part of the individuation process. In successive periods of development, as this process goes on, the person forms a clearer boundary between self and world. He forms a stronger sense of who he is and what he wants, and a more realistic, sophisticated view of the world: what it is like, what it offers him and demands from him. Greater individuation

> allows him to be more separate from the world,
> to be more independent and self-generating. But
> it also gives him the confidence and
> understanding to have more intense attachments
> in the world and to feel more fully a part of
> it.   (1978: 195)

This emphasis on 'separateness', 'independence' and
'self-generation' is the language of the ethic of
individualism, which receives attention elsewhere in
this book. For the present it is worthwhile noting
the claims of at least one commentator, Gilligan
(1979), that the emphasis on the development of
individual identity among developmental theories is
an aspect of gender bias which pervades the
literature. She begins her analysis by referring to
the work of Chodorow (1978), who observes that, in
general, girls are parented by a person of the same
gender while boys are parented by a person of the
opposite gender. The significance of this is that
the identity of boys is built on the perception of
contrast and separateness from their primary
caregiver, while the identity of girls is built upon
the perception of sameness and attachment to their
primary caregiver. Gilligan remarks:

> Consequently, relationships, and particularly
> issues of dependency, are experienced
> differently by women and men. For boys and men,
> separation and individuation are critically tied
> to gender identity since separation from the
> mother is essential for the development of
> masculinity. For girls and women, issues of
> femininity or feminine identity do not depend on
> the achievement of separation from the mother or
> on the progress of individuation. Since
> masculinity is defined through separation while
> femininity is defined through attachment, male
> gender identity is threatened by intimacy while
> female gender identity is threatened by
> separation. Thus males tend to have difficulty
> with relationships, while females tend to have
> problems with individuation. The quality of
> embeddedness in social interaction and personal
> relationships that characterizes women's lives
> in contrast to men's, however, becomes not only
> a descriptive difference but also a
> developmental liability when the milestones of
> childhood and adolescent development in the
> psychological literature are markers of
> increasing separation. Women's failure to

separate then becomes by definition a failure to
develop.   (1979:8-9)

Gilligan then proceeds to cite evidence of the
undervaluing of female characteristics - the concern
with relationships and responsibilities, empathy and
attachment - among developmental theories. For
example, Freud considered the persistence of women's
pre-Oedipal attachment to their mother to be linked
with their failure to resolve completely their
Oedipal feelings and their consequent failure to
develop a strong superego. This developmental
failure in women results (in Freud's view) in their
having little sense of justice:

> The fact that women must be regarded as having
> little sense of justice is no doubt related to
> the predominance of envy in their mental life
> ...'.   (1973b:168)

Another example comes from Jean Piaget, who observed
sex differences in the way children engage in
games. Girls, because of their more flexible
attitude towards rules and their enforcement were
considered to have a less developed legal sense than
boys - which is the cornerstone of moral development.

> (for boys and girls) ... the rule is no longer
> an imperative coming from an adult and accepted
> without discussion, it is a means of agreement
> resulting from co-operation itself. But girls
> are less explicit about this agreement and this
> is our reason for suspecting them of being less
> concerned with legal elaborations. A rule is
> good so long as the game repays it.
> (1977a:78)

Kohlberg too is open to the same criticism.
Gilligan observes that his empirical work, which led
to the formulation of moral development stages, was
based on a sample of boys only. Not surprisingly,
women tend to score lower on Kohlberg's scale than
men. According to Gilligan, this is because the
higher stages of Kohlberg's scale are constructed
from what are traditionally 'male' qualities - the
concern with justice and rights (premised on
individuation) rather than with responsibilities and
relationships.
    The thrust of Gilligan's argument is that
womanhood is rarely equated with mature healthy
adulthood in much of the adult developmental

literature. This is because the healthy personality
is too often portrayed from a male perspective, with
an emphasis on individuation and autonomy.

> The elusive mystery of women's development lies
> in its recognition of the continuing importance
> of attachment in the human life cycle. Woman's
> place in man's life cycle is to protect this
> recognition while the developmental litany
> intones the celebration of separation, autonomy,
> individuation, and natural rights.   (1979:23)

Development as a dialectical process

An alternative to documenting the 'stages' and
'phases' of adult life is to understand development
as an ongoing dialectical process (see Riegel, 1976;
Buss, 1979; Wozniak, 1975; Basseches, 1984). The
basic notion here is that there is a constant
'dialectic' between the changing or developing
person and the changing or evolving society. That
is, the person creates, and is created by the
society in which he/she lives. Accompanying this
notion is the rejection of those psychological
approaches which search for stability, equilibrium
and balance in the life course. The person is
construed as a changing person in a changing world,
and the dialectical approach is very much concerned
with the dynamics of change:

> The preference for an equilibrium model in the
> behavioural sciences has been as firmly
> established as has the preference for abstract
> traits or competencies. Whithout any debate it
> has been taken for granted that a state of
> balance, stability, and rest is more desirable
> than a state of upheaval, conflict and change.
> Thus we have always aimed for a psychology of
> satisfaction but not of excitement. This
> preference has found expression in balance
> theory, equilibrium theory, steady state theory,
> and indirectly in the theory of cognitive
> dissonance. With the possible exception of the
> latter, these interpretations fail to explore
> the fact that every change has to be explained
> by the process of imbalance which forms the
> basis for any movement. Once this prerequisite
> is recognized, stability appears as a transitory
> condition in the stream of ceaseless
> changes.   (Riegel, 1976:690)

One source of such change is the historical change
in one's culture (or sub-culture), the other source
is the change associated with one's age-related
social category (e.g. child, youth, young adult,
elder). Such changes are primarily mediated through
people interacting in everyday life – thus an
investigation of developmental change will entail an
analysis of common, everyday interactions and the
dialogues contained in them.

Riegel's position has much in common with Berger
and Luckmann's (1967) exposition of how personal
identity is shaped, maintained and transmitted
within a given social order. Their analysis offers
a powerful account of how personal identity is a
social construction which, especially in a modern
pluralistic society, is constantly open to change
and transformation. What is meant by the
proposition that personal identity is a social
construction? Put simply, the idea is as follows:

1. We do not have biologically determined
    identities;
2. We are all born into a particular social world
    which has been constructed by humans;
3. We develop a notion of who we are from the way
    'significant' others (e.g. parents) treat us
    (interact with us);
4. These 'significant' others represent the social
    world and mediate it to us.
5. We take on the roles and attitudes of
    significant others, internalise them and make
    them our own;
6. We extend our identification with significant
    others to an identification with society as a
    whole: 'Only by virtue of this generalised
    identification does his own self-identification
    attain stability and continuity. He now has not
    only an identity vis-a-vis this or that
    significant other, but an identity in
    general....'   (1967:153).

Identity, as a social construction, needs to be
maintained through social interaction. The routines
of everyday life serve to confirm the reality of the
world and our place in it. In particular, the
language used in everyday conversations confirms for
us the silent, taken-for-granted world that forms
the foundation of our personal identity. In modern
pluralistic society, however, there is a
multiplicity of world views or realities. Because
there is no common social reality there is (after

primary socialisation) no socially produced stable structure of personal identity. This means that achieving a stable personal identity in modern society becomes an individual, private enterprise. Moreover, the possibility of transforming one's identity is always present. Indeed, one could argue that many life events require a change or re-orientation of identity (e.g. retirement, caring for children, the death of a spouse).

Berger and Luckmann maintain that any transformation of identity requires a process of re-socialisation. In extreme cases, such as with religious conversion, there may be a complete dismantling of one's former identity. This would require the following:

1. Affiliation with the new community;
2. Segregation of the individual from the inhabitants of other 'worlds', especially those from the 'world' being left behind (at least at the initial stages);
3. A reinterpretation of the old 'reality' in terms of the new 'reality' (e.g. 'Now I understand the purpose of my doing such and such ...).

Each of these steps can be recognised as extreme versions of what happens to many adults as they develop new personal, family, work and leisure pursuits. The difference between this analysis and the lifespan development literature is that transformation does not imply a move towards some state of maturity – it simply means change, not improvement. Also, there are no propositions about the regularity and predictability of change – only that personal identity is open to change, subject to the existence of a community of others who maintain the change through discourse in everyday life.

The idea of the malleability of personal identity is both a source of hope and an occasion for despair. Hope, because it means that change is always possible; despair, because it implies that a belief in the real, true, authentic self is a fanciful indulgence.

The studies cited in this chapter represent only a sampling of a rich and diverse field of enquiry. They were chosen to reveal some of the pitfalls in theory and research in adult development. Adult development is, in principle, germane to anyone with an interest in adult education. Too often, however, people with an applied intent will latch on to an easily assimilated theory, one which clearly differentiates and orders the 'phases' or 'stages' of life and which advances an unambiguous account of the process and end point of development. Adult educators may find such theories useful but they need to be wary of the methodological and conceptual difficulties. They also need to be mindful of the impact such theories have on shaping and maintaining conventionally held views about what it means to be a mature, healthy adult.

Chapter Five

COGNITIVE DEVELOPMENTAL PSYCHOLOGY:
PIAGET AND KOHLBERG

Introduction

An interest in adult learning invariably leads to a
desire to understand cognitive changes during
adulthood. In seeking to satisfy this desire the
adult educator is likely to encounter different
models of cognitive development after maturity. One
model, the 'stability' model, assumes that adult
cognition remains essentially stable after
maturity. The result of cognitive progress during
childhood is the attainment of mature forms of
reasoning and thinking which are then applied
throughout the adult years. By contrast, the
'decrement' model postulates that there is a gradual
decrease in the ageing individual's capacity to
utilise and organise information, presumably the
result of some kind of biological deterioration.
Finally, the 'decrement with compensation' model
accepts the notion of biological deterioration, but
also emphasises the compensatory effects of
accumulated experience during adult life
(Labouvie-Vief, 1977).
     The 'decrement' and 'decrement plus
compensation' models are based on research deriving
from a particular tradition in psychology –
psychometric theory and methodology – which focuses
on testing and measuring intellectual abilities.
One of the most influential theories in this
tradition is that proposed by Horn and Cattell
(1966, 1967). They separate intellectual ability
into two general factors labelled 'fluid' and
'crystallised' intelligence. Fluid intelligence is
measured by tests of complex reasoning, memory and
figural relations – tests which are said to be
'culture' fair and thereby linked with universal,
biological development. Crystallised intelligence

is measured by tests on infcrmation storage, verbal
comprehension and numerical reasoning - those sort
of abilities which are normally associated with
experience and acculturation. Horn and Cattell's
research reveals that from the teenage years
onwards, there is a decrement in fluid intelligence
and an increment in crystallised intelligence. The
net result is that intellectual functioning remains
relatively stable with age, there is simply a shift
in the balance between fluid and crystallised
intelligence.

In the psychometric tradition, much of the
debate about adult intellectual capacity has centred
on how to measure and/or interpret the consistent
finding that there is decline with age in
performance on 'fluid' type psychometric tests.
Both Schaie (1965, 1973) and Baltes (1968) draw
attention to the methodological problems associated
with cross-sectional studies - basically that they
wrongly interpret age group differences as
indicators of developmental change (whereas they may
simply indicate generational differences).
Labouvie-Vief (1977, 1980) argues that researchers
are too eager to link performance decrements with
biological ageing, she cites evidence that
performance decrements are mainly monitored among
people in poor health and not among those in good
health, and that it is possible to reverse some
decrements through lifestyle improvements. She also
proposes that there is a need to reconceptualise
what we mean by 'intelligence' in its broader sense
of 'adaptability' and that it is a mistake to think
of intelligence along a single quantitative
dimension where there is no distinction between how
we measure the intelligence and adaptability of
different age groups.

It is at this point that the significance of
Piaget's work becomes apparent. He supplies us with
an alternative conception of cognitive growth, one
which places the emphasis on qualitative rather than
quantitative change. Thus he challenges the view
that children are simply quantitatively diminished
adults - he claims that children progress through
different types of thinking as they develop towards
mature adult thought. Unfortunately Piaget does not
provide us with an account of cognitive development
past the adolescent years. Nevertheless his
approach to childhood cognitive development can be
used as a point of reference for illuminating the
state of things in adulthood. In his description of
cognitive development Piaget postulates a number of

stages through which the person progresses in an invariant sequence. These stages represent qualitatively different ways of making sense, understanding, and constructing a knowledge of the world. Piaget is particularly concerned with documenting the development of a specific type of knowledge - the kind of knowledge which arises from acting in the world and reflecting on our actions and experiences. The following anecdote illustrates what Piaget has in mind:

> One of my friends who is a great mathematician described to me an experience that he had as a child. While counting some pebbles, he arranged them in a line, counted them from left to right, and found that there were ten. He decided to count them from right to left and found there were still ten. He was surprised and delighted, so he changed the shape again. He put them in a circle, counted around the circle, and found there were still ten ... It was a great intellectual experience for him. He had discovered that the sum ten is independent of the order of counting. But unlike their weight, neither the sum nor the order is a property of the pebbles. The sum and the order come from the actions of the subject himself. It was he who introduced the order and it was he who did the counting. So logico-mathematical experience is experience in which the information comes from the subject's own actions and from the coordinations among his actions.
> (Piaget, 1977b:6-7)

It is the emergence of this type of knowledge in the person, logico-mathematical knowledge, that Piaget documents and orders into a sequence of stages, labelled sensory-motor (approx. 0-2 years), pre-operational (approx. 2-6 years), concrete-operational (approx. 7-11 years), and formal-operational (12 years plus). These stages represent qualitatively different ways of making sense, understanding, and constructing a knowledge of the world. For example the earliest stage is characterised by a practical intelligence where the infant learns to act in the world and produce effects. Innate reflexes such as grasping and sucking form the basis of a few rudimentary action patterns that the infant develops. Eventually these action patterns become co-ordinated so that objects which are seen, may then be reached for, grasped, brought to the mouth and sucked. Literally, the world is a place to be grasped and sucked, it is a world of sensations and there is no differentiation between the self, the objects encountered, and one's actions on those objects. Indeed the world and its objects have a reality only if they can be sensed. During this stage these distinctions are gradually acquired and the infant comes to understand that objects have an independent existence. In the pre-operational stage the child can think about objects and events when they are absent. This capacity for representational thought is the foundation for deferred imitation (imitating a person's actions after some time has elapsed), make believe (pretending to do and be various things) and language. Despite these advances, the stage is best characterised by the limitations of the child's thought processes, such as the inability to take the role or view of the other person (egocentrism), the tendency to focus on only one aspect of an object or event when reasoning (centration), the tendency to endow inanimate objects with human qualities (animism)and the propensity to link ideas and things through association only (intuitive thought). In the concrete-operational stage the child has a more coherent and integrated cognitive system which permits an understanding of concepts (such as quantity, length, number, weight, volume) and an understanding of classes and their relationships.

It is the final stage which marks the commencement of mature adult thought. The distinctive mark of the formal-operational child is the capacity to think hypothetically about the 'possible', that is, to think in abstract terms. This is the basis of logical, scientific thinking, but it also leads to an understanding of abstract principles enshrined in the social order (e.g. justice, ethics, moral philosophy). The two experiments outlined in Table 5.1 illustrate some of these capacities.

In the balance beam experiment the concrete-operational child fails to see how distance systematically compensates for weight and how weight systematically compensates for distance. He/she understands the influence of weight and distance alone, but cannot co-ordinate the two. In the chemical solutions experiment the formal-operational child can systematically list all possible combinations and thus be guaranteed of finding the solution. By contrast, the concrete-operational child can systematically test the simple

Table 5.1: Comparison of concrete operations and formal operations on two tasks.

Material	Task	Concrete operations	Formal operations
Balance beam			

Material	Task
Chemical solutions filled with colour-less, odourless liquids.	To produce the colour yellow, know-ing that g + one of, or some combination of 1, 2, 3 and 4 will produce yellow.

Concrete operations:

1 + g
2 + g
3 + g
and some haphazard complex combinations
eg. 1 + 4 + g,
2 + 3 + g.

Formal operations:

Systematically tests all possible combinations until the solution is found.

combinations - but any further attempts are based only on trial and error. The performance of the concrete-operational child is limited by his/her cognitive structure.

There are some propositions in Piaget's theory which trigger the interest of adult educators. Firstly, his outline of the principal stages of cognitive development immediately raises questions concerning the meaning of 'stage' and the relationship between different stages. This is an enquiry worth pursuing because it has relevance for the entire gamut of stage developmental theories. Secondly, his description of the processes which account for development from one stage to the next has implications for our understanding of learning in a more general sense. Finally, his conception of mature adult thought (formal operations) challenges the idea of fundamental cognitive developmental progress during adulthood.

The meaning of 'stages' and their relationships

Flavell (1971, 1972) has completed a thorough analysis of the problems and issues in describing development in terms of a sequence of stages. But firstly, Flavell and Wohlwill provide us with a crisp definition of 'stage'.

> Most typically, the stage concept is invoked to refer to a mode, pattern, or constellation of behaviours (or dispositions towards behaviour) that seems to characterize some definable period in the child's life, be this period specified in terms of chronological age (with the resultant difficulty of taking individual differences in rate of development into account) or in terms of its position in a sequence. The expression 'the stage of infancy', would exemplify the former, while 'the crawling stage' would illustrate the latter use.   (1969:91)

One of the first issues in identifying a stage concerns the range of behaviours it should encompass. In the above definition the 'crawling stage' is quite narrow and specific, while the 'stage of infancy' is general and non-specific. Narrowly defined, purely descriptive stages, risk the charge of being of little interest theoretically, whereas stages which have a high degree of generality are thereby invested with a theoretical status beyond the purely descriptive.

The Freudian stages, mentioned earlier, have a high degree of generality, and they serve to unite quite disparate and seemingly unrelated behaviours. Indeed, this unifying aspect is a characteristic of Piaget's theory and it is arguably a necessary condition for the concept of stage to be at all meaningful. Flavell outlines four components of the stage concept, they are:

1. Qualitative changes - 'Stage to stage development entails qualitative rather than quantitative changes in thinking' (1971:423).

    There are many quantitative changes in development but it would be ludicrous to label them stages (e.g. the 'counting to ten stage' as opposed to the 'counting to twenty stage' or the '100 word vocabulary stage' as opposed to the '2000 word vocabulary stage'). Quantitative changes describe 'less' and 'more' of a particular ability whereas qualitative changes describe a shift to a different type of ability.

2. Abruptness - 'The development of individual stage specific abilities is characteristically abrupt rather than gradual' (1971:425).

    This 'abruptness' criterion raises the issue of whether there is an increase in the functional maturity of an ability within a particular stage (i.e. does the ability develop from an initial level of competence to a more advanced level?). This is an important issue because it determines whether a stage is conceived of as a 'state' or as a 'process'. For Piaget a 'stage' has both these elements: 'A stage thus comprises both a level of preparation, on the one hand, and of achievement, on the other' (1955:35, quoted in Flavell, 1971:428).

3. Concurrence - 'The abilities which define a particular stage develop concurrently, i.e. in synchrony with one another'. (1971:435)

    The notion of concurrence is quite slippery because once the acquisition of an ability is regarded as an extended process it becomes difficult to know what concurrence means. It could mean two abilities commencing at the same time but 'maturing' at different times. Or it could mean two abilities commencing at different times but maturing at the same time.

Whichever of these is the case, there are insurmountable problems in measuring 'concurrence' and the evidence that exists does not seem to support the idea of a tight synchrony in the development of different abilities. In addition, Flavell argues that concurrence is not essential to the stage concept: 'Surely the fact that these items are now functionally interrelated in your head, now comprise a tightly knit cognitive structure, etc., in no way implies that you must have acquired them all simultaneously' (1971:442).

4. Structures - 'Stage specific abilities become organised and interrelated to form cognitive structures.'   (1971:443)

    At its most simple level, a structure will consist of two or more abilities that are interrelated. In addition, these abilities and their relationships are relatively stable and form the underlying basis of a range of superficially distinct behaviours (e.g. the rules we use to construct sentences). Flavell (1971) argues that it is difficult to contest the existence of cognitive structures - cognitive abilities characteristically interact in various ways to form total concepts. The more important issue is not whether 'cognitive structures' exist but how to verify or falsify particular structures.

If we set aside for the moment the problems and issues associated with 'stages' and their measurement, there remains the need to specify the kinds of relationships that exist between different stages. Many developmental theories postulate a sequence of stages, but for a particular sequence to be theoretically interesting the relationship would need to be more than merely temporal. What are the principal ways in which stages may be related? Flavell (1972) documents five such relationships and these are summarised in Table 5.2.

Developmental processes

In explaining the processes of cognitive development Piaget proposes certain mechanisms which are common to all stages. These mechanisms, or, as Piaget

Table 5.2:
A taxonomy of cognitive developmental sequences.

Relationship	Description	Example
1. Addition	Once X_2 has been acquired X_1 continues to be fully and permanently available. X_2 serves mainly to enrich and diversify a person's inventory of responses.	The young child develops a behavioural map of his or her surroundings. However it will be several years before this can be represented symbolically.
2. Substitution	X_2 replaces X_1, i.e. X_1 becomes extinguished as a response.	Initially dreams are believed to be real physical events. This is replaced with the belief that they are mental events with an internal origin.
3. Modification	X_1 and X_2 are different forms or varieties of the same thing. X_2 is an improved, perfected or matured version of X_1.	The infant's sucking scheme comes to distinguish between suckable and non-nourishing and suckable and nourishing.
4. Inclusion	X_1 becomes included in X_2. X_2 is predicated on the development of X_1 so that X_1-X_2 sequence is logically necessary.	Making inferences about the other's perspective is necessary prior to generating listener appropriate communication.
5. Mediation	X_1 is a developmental bridge to X_2. X_1 merely contributes to the initial formation of X_2.	Grasping and manipulating objects is a useful 'bridge' to developing object permanence.

refers to them, 'functional invariants' (Piaget,
1973:62-3), derive from our biological make up. One
such functional invariant is organisation, which is
the tendency to systematise, coordinate or structure
the experience of objects in order to make such
experience meaningful. Constructing 'cognitive
structures' is thus a basic tendency of the
organism. The other 'functional invariant' is
adaptation, which consists of the two processes of
assimilation and accommodation.

Assimilation is the tendency to distort or alter
our encounters with new objects and experiences so
that they fit within our existing understanding of
the world (i.e. our cognitive structure). For
example, the grasping reflex of the infant will be
applied indiscriminately to a range of objects:
large, small, thick, thin, soft and hard. This
represents the infant's attempt to assimilate the
objects of the world to its existing way of
understanding the world. Certain objects may be
actually physically amenable to such distortion
(e.g. plasticine), but most are not. The world has
a way of imposing its reality upon us and we are
bound to 'accommodate' this reality. Accommodation
is the tendency to alter our cognitive structures to
fit the objects we encounter. The infant will thus
begin to differentiate between different types of
objects and the initial primitive grasp will be
replaced by one which is more complex and more
effective in manipulating objects.

The principle in this example extends to what
are considered to be more 'cognitive' acts of the
person: such as forming concepts, developing an
understanding of rules or constructing strategies
for solving problems. The principle is that the
growth of knowledge is based on the interplay
between assimilation and accommodation, between the
person acting on and 'constructing' the world and
the world acting on the person. In this way
cognitive structures are formed, which essentially
are a coherent set of strategies or rules which are
used to understand the world.

In Piaget's account of development, these
cognitive structures (which can be described in
logico-mathematical terms) may be relatively stable
and enduring affairs. That is, the person can apply
them to make sense of the world, consistently and
without contradiction. When this occurs the
cognitive structures are said to be in equilibrium.
However, Piaget asserts that some forms of
equilibrium are 'superior' to others and that

cognitive development proceeds from 'less' to 'more' adequate states of equilibrium. These states of equilibrium constitute the 'stages' of cognitive development previously outlined.

At this point Piaget needs to explain how and why the child moves from lower to higher equilibrium states. In order to do this he incorporates into his system a process which reflects a basic motivational factor in development. He refers to the process as equilibration. In its motivational aspect it refers to a search for better equilibrium, which is a tendency inherent in all healthy organisms. Rotman remarks:

> ... the need for this balance arises endogenously, it is imposed on an individual from within rather than from any source in society, and its satisfaction is a biological necessity essential to the health and well being of the organism. Indeed, for Piaget durable disequilibria constitute pathological organic or mental states   (1977:96).

Thus not only is there an intrinsic need for schemes or cognitive structures to function but they seek to function at the highest possible level of equilibrium. Lower level equilibrium states are indeed a kind of disequilibrium state in that they are only 'equilibrated' with respect to a limited field of application. Any attempt to extend the field of application will lead to conflicting and competing subschemes, the child will encounter inconsistency and contradiction in his/her experience which will ultimately be resolved by a reorganisation of his/her cognitive structure at a higher level. This is the mechanistic aspect of equilibration; when contradictions arise through the inadequacies of lower level equilibrium states then cognitive progress will ensue.

An experiment of Doise (et al) illustrates this process quite nicely. They used a standard Piagetian test for the conservation of length:

> 'A child who does not attain conservation of length admits that two equal rulers, whose ends perceptually coincide, are of equal length, but when one of the rulers is displaced so that one of its tips is no more in line with the tip of the other ruler, the non-conserving child thinks that one ruler is now longer than the other.' (1976:245)

When children claim that, after a displacement, one ruler is longer than the other, the typical adult correction is to say 'no, the top ruler is further here, but the bottom ruler is further there, so both are the same length'. However, Doise (et al) shows that a more effective intervention is to point to the opposite end of the other ruler and say 'I think this ruler is longer, you see, it goes further there'. The ingenuity of this experiment is that children were provided with a model of reasoning similar to their own but which led to a different judgement. Presumably this highlighted the contradictions inherent in their inability to conserve length, and the perception of this contradiction acted as a springboard for cognitive progress. Conflict and contradiction then, lie at the heart of cognitive development.

To sum up, Piaget's view of the development of knowledge is that fundamentally invariant cognitive processes (organisation, assimilation, accommodation, equilibration) progressively produce qualitatively different equilibrium states, or 'stages' through which the child passes in his or her development towards adult forms of reasoning.

To reiterate, there are a number of ways in which Piaget's work is relevant to an understanding of adult learning and development. His most pertinent legacies in this respect are:

1. The emphasis on qualitative rather than quantitative developmental changes in cognition (and his related 'structuralist' approach to cognitive development).
2. The importance attached to the active role of the person in constructing his or her knowledge (with the implication that learning through activity is more meaningful).
3. A conception of mature, adult thought (i.e. formal operations).

Each of these legacies is apparent in research and theory which attempts to extend Piaget's work to the years beyond adolescence, and/or which applies his approach to different developmental domains (such as the development of morality, or social cognition). They are also apparent, however, as focal points in the literature which offers a critical appraisal of his work.

Critique of Piaget

Piagetian theory has received a great deal of criticism on conceptual and methodological grounds. There are the usual charges that his 'experiments' are badly controlled and incompletely reported – that he fails to provide precise and clear details of his procedure, that he varies his procedure from subject to subject, that he omits rudimentary information about his subjects, and that he omits checks on the face validity and reliability of his stage classification procedures. In addition he is said to have a tendency to over-interpret his data and to leave large gaps between his theory construction and the empirical findings he is writing about. Some of the conceptual difficulties of his theory are implicit in the foregoing analysis of the concepts of 'stage' and 'sequence'. It is apparent from this analysis that it is difficult, if not impossible, to establish empirically that two or more cognitive acquisitions do in fact emerge in a particular chronological order in an individual's life.

All the above criticisms deal with conceptual and methodological difficulties within the framework of Piaget's theory. Two important criticisms, however, strike at the core of his work. The first of these relates to a tension between two features of Piaget's theory – his structuralism and his constructivism. The second concerns the adequacy of formal operations as a complete account of mature, adult thought.

Piaget's 'structuralist' approach is exemplified by his description of a sequence of 'stable' cognitive structures in the course of development. His 'constructivist' approach is to be found in his explanation of the processes of cognitive development – processes which explain change rather than stability. The person, through interaction with the environment, constructs his/her knowledge through the interplay between assimilation and accommodation. Now the issue is whether structuralism or constructivism dominates in Piaget's work. There are two lines of argument which suggest that structuralism dominates. One of these is expressed by Basseches:

> ...while it is relatively easy to see how the constructivist model operates in Piaget's description of infants' cognition, it gets harder and harder as one moves up the

developmental scale. More and more,
assimilation seems to dominate over
accommodation, so that finally we have clear
explanations and examples of how adolescents
apply their formal operational structures to
solving problems, but we have no such
explanations or examples of how new experiences
force adolescents to construct new forms of
reasoning that transcend the limits of their
formal analyses. The formal operational system
seems so abstract that it can be applied to any
kind of problem without accommodation.
(1984:52)

In Piaget's scheme of things there is no further
structural change after the attainment of formal
operations. Formal operational thought is a closed
system structure which can assimilate any
experience. According to Basseches, this implies
that the dialectical interplay of assimilation and
accommodation ends with formal operational thought -
a view which he, and others (Riegel, 1973;
Buck-Morss, 1975) reject.
    The Piagetian approach has been applied to the
years beyond adolescence but the research has mainly
focused on whether, and how, formal operational
thought is generalised, extended and maintained in
adulthood (see Long, 1983 for a summary). Another
line of enquiry has highlighted the limitations of
formal operations in describing mature adult
thought. A common thread in this enquiry is that
mature adult cognition is characterised by the
ability to fit abstract thinking into the concrete
limitations of everyday life. Labouvie-Vief
captures the spirit of this enquiry:

    While the theme of youth is flexibility, the
    hallmark of adulthood is commitment and
    responsibility. Careers must be started,
    intimacy bonds formed, children raised. In
    short, in a world of a multitude of logical
    possibilities, one course of action must be
    adopted. This conscious commitment to one
    pathway and the deliberate disregard of other
    logical choices may mark the onset of adult
    cognitive maturity....

    The pure logic of youth may, of course, serve a
    local or temporary adaptive value, and therefore
    its importance should not be denigrated. It
    permits a circulatory exercise of operatory

> schemes that are to be put to pragmatic use
> later on. It thus helps to guarantee the
> flexibility demanded of mature adult
> adaptation. This is our first proposed
> conclusion: adulthood brings structural change,
> not just in the perfection of logic, but in its
> reintegration with pragmatic necessities.
> (1980:153)

This need to take into account pragmatic necessities
may require the ability to tolerate contradiction
and ambiguity, which, according to Riegel, is a
feature of adult thought:

> The mature person needs to achieve a new
> apprehension and an effective use of
> contradictions in operations and thoughts.
> Contradictions should no longer be regarded as
> deficiencies that have to be straightened out by
> formal thinking but, in a confirmative manner,
> as the very basis of all activities. In
> particular, they form the basis for any
> innovative and creative work. Adulthood and
> maturity represent the period in life during
> which the individual knowingly reappraises the
> role of formal, i.e. noncontradictory thought
> and during which he may succeed again (as the
> young child has unknowingly succeeded in his
> 'primitive dialectic') to accept contradictions
> in his actions and thoughts ('scientific
> dialectic').   (1975:101)

In the above examples, formal operations is deemed
to be limited by its abstractness and removal from
everyday problem-posing and solving. It is a type
of reasoning which is correctly applied to a very
narrow range of problems, but which can only play a
subordinate role in efforts to solve the concrete
problems of adult life.
   Piaget's emphasis on an invariant (and
universal) sequence of stages leading to mature
formal operational thought and his apparent
disregard for psychological phenomena which defy
structural analysis (feelings, beliefs, values,
imagination, desire) has attracted a flood of what
may be called 'ideology' critiques. This body of
criticism is summarised and evaluated by Broughton
in the last article of a series of five articles on
Piaget's theory. Basically, Piaget's theory is
portrayed as being an outgrowth of liberal ideology.

> The Piagetian developmental theory is criticized
> as a form of ideological legitimization which
> supports the current organisation and political
> stratification of society and rationalises the
> extant socialisation processes reproducing the
> present social order, by showing them to be
> accurate reflections of 'natural',
> quasi-biological sequences of individual
> growth. From this critical perspective, both
> the sequence of structures and the theory of it
> represent purely <u>conventional</u> meaning systems,
> with no clear objectivity. The very concept of
> 'development' can even be construed as a
> reification of history deriving from the
> nineteenth century ideology of progress.
> (1981:387)

This is a forceful criticism but, on first
encounter, it seems quite remote from Piaget's
project. Nevertheless, it is possible to illustrate
the validity and relevance of such a criticism by
following the subsequent application of Piaget's
theory to what is known as 'social cognition' -
which emcompasses the development of concepts of
society, concepts of morality, concepts of politics,
etc. By far the best known and often cited research
in this area is that of Kohlberg on the development
of moral judgement. This will be treated below as
an application of Piaget's structuralist theory; and
as an illustration of how the theory can be used to
support prevailing social institutions by
considering them to be a 'natural' outgrowth of
mature adult reasoning.

Kohlberg's research on moral judgement

Kohlberg (1969, 1971, 1973) considers moral
judgement to be a specific case of general cognitive
development. His research technique is to present
subjects with a moral dilemma, ask them to make a
decision about the correct course of action, and
then question them about the reasons for their
decision. He is not concerned with the actual
decisions or conclusions of the subjects, but with
the way they reason about the moral issues involved
(i.e. the structure of their moral reasoning). He
devised a number of moral dilemmas, and the best
known of these is reproduced below.

In Europe, a woman was near death from cancer.
There was one drug that the doctors thought

might save her. It was a form of radium that a
chemist in the same town had recently
discovered. The drug was expensive to make, but
the chemist was charging ten times what the drug
cost him to make. He paid $200 for the radium
and charged $2,000 for a small dose of the
drug. The sick woman's husband, Heinz, went to
everyone he knew to borrow the money, but he
could only get together about $1,000, which is
half of what it cost. He told the chemist that
his wife was dying and asked him to sell it
cheaper or let him pay later. The chemist said,
'No, I discovered the drug and I'm going to make
money from it'. So Heinz got desperate and
broke into the man's store to steal the drug for
his wife. Should the husband have done that?
Why?

To reiterate, Kohlberg is not at all concerned with
whether subjects believe Heinz should or should not
have stolen the drug. The critical dimension is the
reasoning the subjects use to justify their
decision. Kohlberg (1969) found that the ability to
reason about moral issues is acquired in the course
of development and can be described in terms of a
sequence of six stages, grouped into three levels
(see Table 5.3). He claims that the relationship
between the various stages of his 'sequence' of
moral stages is similar to that postulated by Piaget
in his cognitive developmental theory.

A cognitive-developmental theory of moralisation
holds that there is a sequence of moral stages
for the same basic reasons that there are
cognitive or logico-mathematical stages, that is
because cognitive structural reorganisations
toward the more equilibrated occur in the course
of interaction between the organism and the
environment.   (1971:183)

Thus Kohlberg portrays his stages as representing a
hierarchy of structures which become progressively
more differentiated as development occurs. He makes
several claims about these stages:

1.   They imply an invariant sequence, that is, the
      order of progression through them is the same
      for each child. However, there may be
      individual differences in the speed of
      progression and there is always the possibility
      of becoming fixated at any stage.

Table 5.3: Kohlberg's stages of moral development

Level	Stages
I. Preconventional level At this level the child is responsive to cultural rules and labels of good and bad, right and wrong, but interprets these labels in terms of either the physical or hedonistic consequences of action (punishment, reward, exchange of favours), or in terms of the physical power of those who enunciate the rules and labels.	**Stage 1:** The punishment and obedience orientation. The physical consequences of action determine its goodness or badness regardless of the human meaning or value of these consequences. Avoidance of punishment and unquestioning deference to power are valued in their own right, not in terms of respect for an underlying moral order supported by punishment and authority (the latter being stage 4). **Stage 2:** The instrumental relativist orientation. Right action consists of that which instrumentally satisfies one's own needs and occasionally the needs of others. Human relations are viewed in terms like those of the market place. Elements of fairness, of reciprocity, and of equal sharing are present, but they are always interpreted in a physical, pragmatic way. Reciprocity is a matter of "you scratch my back and I'll scratch yours", not of loyalty, gratitude, or justice.
II. Conventional level At this level, maintaining the expectations of the individual's family, group or nation is perceived as valuable in its own right, regardless of immediate and obvious consequences. The attitude is not only one of conformity to personal expectations and social order, but of loyalty to it, of actively maintaining, supporting and justifying the order, and of identifying with the persons or group involved in it.	**Stage 3:** The interpersonal concordance or "good boy - nice girl" orientation. Good behaviour is that which pleases or helps others and is approved by them. There is much conformity to stereotypical images of what is majority or "natural" behaviour. Behaviour is frequently judged by intention - "he means well" becomes important for the first time. One earns approval by being "nice". **Stage 4:** The "law and order" orientation. This is orientation towards authority, fixed rules, and the maintenance of social order. Right behaviour consists of doing one's duty, showing respect for authority and maintaining the given social order for its own sake.

Table 5.3: Kohlberg's stages of moral development (cont'd)

Level	Stages
III. Postconventional, autonomous or principled level At this level, there is a clear effort to define moral values and principles which have validity and application apart from the authority of the group or persons holding these principles, and apart from the individual's own identification with these groups.	**Stage 5:** The social-contact legalistic orientation, generally with utilitarian overtones. Right action tends to be defined in terms of general individual rights and standards which have been critically examined and agreed upon by the whole society. There is a clear awareness of the relativism of personal values and opinions and a corresponding emphasis upon procedural rules for reaching consensus. Aside from what is constitutionally and democratically agreed upon right is a matter of personal "values" and "opinions". The result is an emphasis upon the "legal point of view", but with an emphasis upon the possibility of changing law in terms of rational considerations of social utility (rather than freezing it in terms of stage 4 "law and order"). Outside the legal realm, free agreement and contract is the binding element of obligation. This is the "official" morality of the American government and constitution. **Stage 6:** The universal ethical principle orientation. Right is defined by the decision of conscience in accord with self-chosen ethical principles appealing to logical comprehensiveness, universality and consistency. These principles are abstract and ethical (the Golden Rule, the categorical imperative); they are not concrete moral rules like the Ten Commandments. At heart, these are universal principles of justice, of the reciprocity and equality of human rights, and of respect for the dignity of human beings as individual persons.

2. Stages are defined in terms of 'structured wholes', i.e. 'total ways of thinking, not attitudes towards particular situations' (Kohlberg, 1971:169).
3. The stage concept implies a universality of sequence regardless of cultural conditions. This is in line with Kohlberg's argument against the conception of moral development as being another aspect of socialisation. It should be noted that an individual is usually not entirely at any one stage. Typically, as children develop they are partly in their major stage (about 50% of their ideas) partly in the stage into which they are moving, and partly in the stage they have just left behind.
4. Finally, Kohlberg's claim for the superiority of higher stages of moral judgement is based upon the recognition of their formal properties and the assertion that it is these formal properties which constitute moral judgement proper, i.e. they are criteria which make judgements moral. He claims that he has succeeded in isolating the structure or form of morality from its content:

> ... we define morality in terms of the formal character of a moral judgement, method, or point of view, rather than in terms of its content... But we claim that the formal definition of morality only works when we recognise that there are developmental levels of moral judgement which increasingly approximates the philosopher's moral form. This recognition shows us a) that there are criteria which make judgements moral; b) that these are only fully met by the most mature stages of judgement, so that; c) our mature stages of judgements are more moral (in the formalist sense, more morally adequate) than less mature stages.   (1971:215)

It is not appropriate here to provide an exhaustive account of the various criticisms of Kohlberg's theory. A dominant theme, however, is that Kohlberg does an injustice to the very concept of morality by treating it in such a formal and abstract way (Morelli, 1978; Habermas, 1979; Buck-Morss, 1975; Youniss, 1978; Sullivan, 1977; Peters, 1971; Henry, 1980). For example, Sullivan (1977) argues that abstract formalisms are, in themselves, neither moral nor immoral, and that a fusion of the abstract

and the concrete is necessary for moral commitment.
In a similar line of argument Peters contends that
moral judgements cannot be said to be 'superior'
without reference to some culturally specific value:

> A further point must be made, too, about any
> moral system in which justice is regarded as the
> fundamental principle: it cannot be applied
> without a view, deriving from considerations
> other than those of justice, about what is
> important. This point can be demonstrated only
> very briefly, but it is one of cardinal
> importance. When we talk about what is just or
> unjust, we are applying the formal principle of
> reason - that no distinctions should be made
> without relevant differences, either to
> questions of distribution, when we are concerned
> about the treatment which different people are
> to receive, or to commutative situations, when
> we are concerned not with comparisons but with
> questions of desert, as in punishment. In all
> such cases some criterion has to be produced by
> reference to which the X treatment is to be
> based on relevant considerations. There must
> therefore be some further evaluative premise in
> order to determine relevance. Without such a
> premise, no decisions can be made about what is
> just on any substantive issue. In determining,
> for instance, what a just wage is, relevant
> differences must be determined by reference to
> what people need, to what they contribute to the
> community, to the risk involved, and so on. To
> propose any such criteria involves
> evaluation.   (1971:263-4)

Thus the 'highest' stage of moral development does
not lead 'naturally' to justice, as Kohlberg would
have us believe. This is because the concept of
justice implies an act or a decision which is either
just or unjust - it does not exist as an
abstraction, unrelated to concrete action. The
development of moral judgement involves more than
progress in the purely contemplative awareness of
different reasons for/against a course of action.
For the term 'moral judgement' to have meaning, it
must refer to values and beliefs and these are
acquired through experiencing a <u>particular</u>
socio-historical world.
    That Kohlberg's theory supports established
social institutions is demonstrated by his
interpretation of a phenomenon he labels 'adolescent

relativism'. This is where the adolescent questions the inevitability and 'naturalness' of existing social institutions. Gilligan and Kohlberg (1978) describe this phenomenon:

> However, while formal operations are thus a necessary prerequisite for principled moral reasoning, they also make possible the questioning of morality itself in a way hitherto inconceivable... The hallmark of the relativist is the unease he manifests when asked to make a moral judgement. The terms <u>right</u> and <u>wrong</u> stick in his throat, and his typical response is either to question their meaning or to assert their meaninglessness. Such questioning is metaethical in that it stands outside the realm of normative ethical judgement and inquires into its premises.... Rejecting conventional moral reasoning on the basis of a relativistic awareness that any given society's definition of right and wrong, however legitimate, is only one among many, both in fact and in theory, these adolescents, instead of moving ahead from Stage 4 to Stage 5, reverted to what sounded like a resurrected Stage 2 moral philosophy of instrumental hedonism.   (1978:126-27)

Kohlberg and Gilligan cite the following response to the Heinz dilemma as an example of the relativist thinking of the adolescent:

> 'It depends on how he is oriented morally. If he thinks it's worse to steal than to let his wife die, then it would be wrong if he did it. It's all relative; what I would do is steal the drug. I can't say that's right or wrong or that it's what everyone should do.'   (1971:1073)

However, this apparent regression of the adolescent into moral nihilism is eventually replaced by a more 'mature' moral developmental stage:

> The forces of development that led 20% from upstanding convention to moral nihilism eventually set them all to rights. Every single one of the <u>retrogressors</u> had returned by age 25 to the moral fold, with more Stage 5 social-contract principle and less Stage 4 convention than in high school. In sum, this 20% were among the highest group at high school,

> the lowest in college, and again among the
> highest at age 25. Moral relativism and
> nihilism, no matter how extensive, seemed to be
> a transitional attitude in the movement from
> conventional to principled morality.
> (1978:129)

Now on Kohlberg's account this extreme relativism of
the adolescent is eventually replaced by a more
mature and stable form of moral judgement, one which
allows a commitment to be made. However, it is not
at all clear that Kohlberg has identified a more
'advanced' cognitive alternative to the relativism
characteristic of adolescents. Arguably the
'principled morality' referred to above is nothing
more than an elaborate and cognitively advanced set
of arguments which serve the purpose of legitimating
existing social institutions. In connection with
this: why is it that adolescent relativism is
inevitably replaced by a (morally principled)
commitment to the social institutions of one's
culture? This is a question incapable of solution
within the cognitive structuralist framework.
Because social institutions are arbitrary, in the
sense that they rest entirely upon social
convention, it makes no sense to explain our
commitment to them solely in terms of our capacity
for higher order reasoning. Some additional
analysis is necessary, one which takes into account
the way in which our feelings, beliefs, attitudes
and values are shaped by forces outside the domain
of cognition.
    On balance, some features of cognitive
developmental psychology are helpful and others
unhelpful for an understanding of adult learning and
development. Among the helpful features are the
idea of qualitative developmental change and the
notion that knowledge is constructed through the
person interacting with the environment. Among the
less helpful features are the proposition that
'formal operations' constitutes the end point of
development and the belief that cognitive
development is the cornerstone for all aspects of
development.

Chapter Six

LEARNING STYLES

Introduction

'Cognitive style', 'learning style' and 'conceptual
style' are related terms which refer to an
individual's characteristic and consistent approach
to organising and processing information. The idea
that people have different learning styles is
enticing for adult educators. Firstly, it
highlights the importance of learning processes
(rather than teaching techniques), and it thereby
raises questions concerning the ideal distribution
of power and control among teachers and learners.
Secondly, it is an egalitarian concept because it
focuses on people's strengths and weaknesses so that
the operative term desribing learners becomes
'different' rather than 'bad' 'poor' 'average'
'good' and 'very good'.
   There have been numerous attempts to classify
the basic ways in which cognitive or learning styles
differ. Messick (1978) identifies nineteen types of
learning style, each type being supported by a range
of research articles and theoretical papers, and
Smith (1984) tabulates seventeen learning style
inventories. Squires (1981) observes that cognitive
styles are typically represented as polar opposites
of a single dimension so that a person is described
as field dependent or independent, reflective or
impulsive, serialist or holist, a converger or a
diverger, and so on. These varied approaches to
cognitive style should not be seen as mutually
exclusive, rather they support the reasonable
expectation that people differ in their learning
styles in a number of ways. Because of this it
would be naive to expect that adult educators could
systematically design and deliver a course to fit
the learning style needs of their students. This

chapter, in part, addresses the issue of how learning style information should be used in the adult classroom. However, this will be done in the context of describing and evaluating two dominant approaches to categorising cognitive styles, the field dependence/independence dimension identified by Witkin, and the Learning Style Inventory developed by Kolb and Fry.

Field dependence and field independence

The terms 'field dependence' and 'field independence' are associated with the program of research triggered by Witkin's (1950) seminal report on individual differences in the influence of context in making simple perceptual judgements. He found that the perceptual judgements of some people are consistently influenced by context, while for others the context has little or no influence. In an early experiment he used a completely darkened room. All the subject could see was a luminous rod surrounded by a luminous square frame. Both the rod and frame could be independently tilted, clockwise or counterclockwise, around a common focal point. The subject was required to adjust the rod so it appeared vertical in the presence of a tilted surrounding frame. Some people could do this quite accurately irrespective of the tilt of the surrounding frame (field independent people). Others adjusted the rod to 'vertical' by aligning it with the surrounding frame, even when the frame was tilted by as much as 30 degrees! (field dependent people).

Figure 6.1
The performance of extreme field independent (a)
and field dependent (b) subjects in Witkin's (1950)
rod and frame test.

(a)   (b)

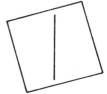
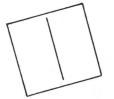

In another version of this test, seated subjects were required to adjust their body to an upright position in a tilted room. Similar results were obtained: some subjects reported they were upright, when in fact they were tilted 30 degrees, while other subjects correctly adjusted themselves to the upright position without being influenced by the tilted room.

Witkin claims that these tests, and similar ones, measure a common factor: the ability to separate figure from context. He eventually developed a pencil and paper test, called the embedded figures test, designed to measure this general ability. In this test the subject is asked to locate a simple figure in a complex design. Once again some people find this task easy and complete it quickly (field independent), while others find it difficult and take longer to complete the test (field dependent). Witkin found a correlation between performance on the rod and frame and body adjustment tests. It is correlations such as these which led him to argue for the existence of different cognitive styles:

> ...the common denominator underlying individual differences in performance in all these tasks is the extent to which a person is able to deal with a part of a field separately from the field as a whole, or the extent to which he is able to disembed items from organised context – to put it in everyday language, the extent to which he is analytical. At one extreme of the performance range, perception is strongly dominated by the prevailing field; we speak of this mode of perception as field dependent. At the other extreme, the perception of an item is relatively independent of the surrounding field, and we refer to this mode of perception as field independent. (1978:42)

One may object that Witkin's tests measure an aspect of general intelligence and therefore add very little to our understanding of cognitive capacities. In this connection it is important to note that field independence/dependence does not represent a continuum from 'better to worse', as indicated by the observation that for some tasks the relatively field dependent person performs more accurately. However, there is some substance to this claim because of persistent evidence that field independents perform better than field dependents on

91

<u>cognitive</u> tasks. Thus Witkin's cognitive style
dimension is, at least, an ingredient of general
intelligence; but it is much more than this, as
demonstrated by numerous studies correlating field
independence/dependence with a host of personal
characteristics, social interaction patterns, and
life choices. The impact of these studies is that
the concept of cognitive style has been extended
from a narrow description of perceptual capacities
to a more global description of different ways of
knowing the world. For example, there are studies
reporting how field dependents rely on a social
frame of reference to formulate their beliefs,
attitudes and feelings, and self concept; that they
make fewer self references in their speech; that
they adapt their rate of speech to the rate of the
person to whom they are communicating; that they are
more sensitive to social cues; that they like to be
with people; that they are better liked; that they
prefer to be physically closer to others, and so
forth. It is these associations with cognitive
style that accounts for the interest of educators in
the concept. Witkin et al (1977) provided the first
and most comprehensive analysis of the educational
implications of cognitive styles. I have adapted
and tabulated this analysis in Table 6.1. The table
contains a summary of research findings which relate
cognitive style to aspects of education; how
students learn, how teachers teach, student-teacher
interaction, and career and educational planning.
On each of these aspects there is a difference
between the strategies, choices, and outcomes for
field dependents and field independents. For
example, the table indicates how the process of
learning is fundamentally different for people with
different cognitive styles. Thus field dependents
are responsive to external reinforcement, they rely
on externally provided structure, they focus on
salient cues when identifying concepts, and they are
better at learning and remembering social material.
The sample of the research findings in the table has
implications for teacher training, educational
guidance and counselling, learner induction, the
streaming or grouping of students, and vocational
preparation. But the implications are not clear cut
and they depend on judgements of efficacy and
value. Using the table as a guideline I will now
address some of the issues in connecting educational
practice with cognitive styles.

Table 6.1: The educational implications of cognitive styles

	Field dependent	Field independent
How students learn		
1. Effect of reinforcement	– External reinforcement more salient.	– Learn more under conditions of intrinsic motivation.
2. Use of mediators in learning	– Rely on externally provided structure, therefore need assistance with unorganised material.	– More likely to structure ambiguous material.
3. Learning of concepts	– Tend to focus on salient cues only – but their strategy can be altered with instruction.	– Tend to sample the entire array of cues (hypothesis testing approach).
4. Learning social material	– Better at learning and remembering social material.	– Need assistance in focusing on social material.
How teachers teach		
1. Methods	– Prefers discussion method and situations which allow interactions with students.	– Prefers lecture and discovery methods, situations which are more impersonal and cognitive.
2. Techniques	– Avoids negative feedback and evaluation.	– Emphasises the need to correct errors and provide negative evaluation where appropriate.
3. Teaching environment	– Prefers rapport, participation, warm and personal environment.	– Shows strength in the organisation and guidance of student learning.

Table 6.1: The educational implications of cognitive styles (cont'd)

	Field dependent	Field independent
Education and career planning		
1. Educational/ vocational interests, choices and achievements	Interpersonal domains which require social skills such as elementary school teaching, social sciences, rehabilitation counselling, welfare.	Analytic and impersonal domains such as physical and biological sciences, mathematics, engineering, technical and mechanical activities.
2. Interests and choices within educational/ vocational areas	Favour specialisations with a 'people' emphasis eg. clinical psychology, psychiatric nursing, social studies teacher.	Favour specialisations which are impersonal and require cognitive skills, eg. experimental psychology, surgical nursing, natural science teaching.
3. Making choices and changing areas	More undecided about occupational choice and less committed to their choice. Shift their college majors away from impersonal and cognitive domains.	Concerned with occupational planning, more specialised vocational interests. Shift their college majors away from personal and social domains.
Student teacher interaction	When teachers and students are matched then: - they view one another more positively - teachers evaluate the performance and intellects of students higher - the goal of the interaction is more likely to be achieved The positive extremes of matching are the result of shared interests, shared personality characteristics, and shared modes of communication. Teachers need to adapt their teaching strategies to the needs of dissimilar students.	

Malleability of cognitive styles

If cognitive styles are unalterable and there is a
fixed relationship between cognitive styles and
learning strategies, then there is little scope for
helping learners overcome the limitations of their
style. Fortunately, on first inspection, this does
not seem to be the case. Witkin et al (1977) review
a number of studies which show that cognitive style,
or at least its behavioural correlates, can be
modified. For example research indicates that the
relative superiority of field dependents in learning
and remembering material with a social context is
due principally to their selective attention to this
material – field independents do just as well when
their attention is focused on such material. In a
similar manner the relative inferiority of field
dependents in using hypothesis testing procedures in
concept learning can be overcome by providing them
with some simple directions on how to use this
approach. Studies like these reveal that the impact
of cognitive style on learning is modifiable. The
implication for teachers is that they should be
aware of learners' cognitive styles and apply
corrective intervention where appropriate.
   Witkin and his colleagues assert that individual
differences in field dependence/independence are
primarily due to socialisation. This suggests that
they are, at least in principle, modifiable through
education or training. However, an early
longitudinal study (Witkin et al, 1967) illustrates
the stability of cognitive style, especially during
the period 17–24 years of age. Chickering is
incredulous that this should be so:

> It is difficult for me to believe that change
> does not occur on the field dependence dimension
> during the college years and that such changes
> are not related to differences in college
> experiences and activities ...If no change
> occurred in field dependence and if no
> relationships to educational experiences and
> activities were found, it would mean that the
> field dependence versus independence
> characteristic has a stability among young
> adults that is not shared by several other
> similar variables.   (1978:81)

This issue of the modifiability of cognitive style
is likely to persist because it has implications for
how best to provide advice and guidance to

learners. If cognitive styles are stable and fixed then teaching intervention can only be cosmetic - under such circumstances it is best to adapt to the 'natural' inclinations of the learner (for example, attempt to match teaching and learning styles, develop alternative learning activities for people with different styles, guide people into those options to which they are suited). If, however, cognitive styles proved to be highly malleable then intervention can take a more active form (assist students to diversify their learning strategies, encourage option choices outside a student's dominant style).

Cognitive style as a bi-polar dimension

One attraction of a cognitive style approach is that it offers an alternative to the grading of student potential from 'better' to 'worse' along some quantitative dimension like intelligence. Intelligence is something one has 'more' or 'less' of, but this does not apply to cognitive style:

> ...with regard to value judgements, cognitive styles are bi-polar. This characteristic is of particular importance in distinguishing cognitive styles from intelligence and other ability dimensions. To have more of an ability is better than to have less of it. With cognitive styles, on the other hand, each pole has adaptive value under special circumstances, and so may be judged positively in relation to those circumstances. (Witkin et al, 1977:16)

The phrase 'adaptive value under special circumstances' is crucial here. It warns us that 'cognitive styles' are not to be read as different ways of acquiring the same kind of knowledge. Research indicates that different types of knowledge are 'more' or 'less' accessible to people with different cognitive styles. Table 6.1 indicates differences in the types of educational and vocational achievements associated with being field dependent/independent - field independents do best with the analytical and impersonal domains such as the physical and biological sciences, mathematics, engineering, technical and mechanical activities; and field dependents do best with interpersonal domains requiring social skills, such as elementary school teaching, the social sciences and welfare. But is there a status difference in the knowledge associated with these different domains and areas of work? I think that there is, and that in the current scheme of things field independence is valued more highly that field dependence. Field independence is associated with abstract and analytical thinking, which are important criteria for high status knowledge. It is also linked with better performance on tests of intelligence and other cognitive tests. Field independents are said to structure ambiguous material more effectively and identify and form concepts more readily. To sum, the skills and qualities associated with field independence appear to be those that society at large values more highly (in this respect it is important to note that females are, at least marginally, more likely to be field dependent). Even in the arena of adult education field independents fare more favourably than field dependents - they are more capable of dealing with a lack of clear direction (i.e. self direction) and they learn more under conditions of intrinsic motivation which Knowles claims is a feature of the adult as opposed to the child learner.

Thus the notion of cognitive style, in its field dependence/independence form does little to liberate the learner from value judgements concerning worthwhile knowledge and worthwhile abilities. The position is exacerbated by the tendency to talk only of 'field independents' or 'field dependents' as if they were mutually exclusive and exhaustive categories into which all learners could be neatly sorted. This tendency is understandable because the dominant research technique is to make comparisons between the extremes of the bi-polar dimension and thus document the limits of the differences between the two cognitive styles. But Witkin clearly indicates that the scores on tests of field independence/dependence form a continuous distribution. If this distribution is normal, then we would expect most people to have styles which reflect both field dependence and field independence. Given this, it is only a short step to acknowledging that in one context a person could be field dependent and in another, field independent. This is the argument advanced by Wapner.

> 'I maintain that [cognitive styles] are not
> independent of the context in which they operate
> and should not be defined as such... for
> example, there may be students who are more

field dependent in the presence of an aggressive teacher and relatively less field dependent in the presence of a submissive teacher. To characterise people as occupying a range on the field dependence versus field independence dimension, with their manifest bahaviour depending on the particular environmental context involves a significant reconceptualisation.' (1978:75-6)

This is a conceptualisation worth embracing because it is appropriate for the bulk of learners and it avoids the dangers associated with moulding cognitive style into an ideal typology.

Match/mis-match of styles

Table 6.1 sets out some of the positive aspects of matching the styles of teachers and students. But Wapner (1978), quite rightly, challenges the educational benefits of matching cognitive styles:

'...with a match in cognitive style there is a greater mutual attraction of student and teacher, greater communication through use of similar communication modes, and greater understanding and creation of good atmosphere for learning. But is this the kind of environment that is optimal for learning?...Is an environment optimal if it conforms to the students expectations? Is an environment optimal if the student and teacher have understanding because they share similarity of viewpoint? A powerful argument can be made that opposition, contradiction and obstacles are necessary conditions for individual development and creativity'. (1978:77-8)

Wapner's comments are supported by the view, especially among cognitive developmental psychologists (see Doise, 1978) that conflict is an important trigger for development. The argument is that the limitations of one's perspective only become apparent when opposing perspectives are encountered. Indeed, learning and development may be regarded as processes whereby initially alien experiences or contradictory observations become understandable through changes in the person. There are, of course, many claims and counter claims regarding such a view, but most practitioners would agree that at least some unsettling experience is a good ingredient for effective learning. These considerations alone are sufficient to prevent one from rigorously matching cognitive styles, but there are two others worth mentioning. First there is the question of whether moulding cognitive styles, in any global sense, is at all possible. I argued in the immediately preceding section that the field dependence/independence dimension forms a continuous distribution and that most people occupy a range on that distribution. The upshot of this is that it makes no sense to try and 'match' the cognitive style of a teacher and a group of students - variations within the group and among the tasks set for the learners would pre-empt this. Secondly, there is the general question of whether education necessarily entails a broadening of the person. To what extent should educators demand that learners step outside the confines of their own skills and capacities and explore new ground? The argument here is that the person capable of learning a variety of things in different ways is better able to adapt to changed circumstances because they have learnt how to learn - which is often professed to be the most cherished outcome of the educational experience.

Cognitive styles and adult learning

Chickering (1978) illustrates how contract learning and programmed learning (which are both alternatives to traditional instruction and are associated with adult education) miss the target when it comes to cognitive styles. Neither of them are suited to one style or the other. Contract learning, for example, provides an opportunity for interaction (which suits field dependents) but it is largely self-referent in the sense that the starting point for learning is the self (which poses difficulties for field dependents). In a similar way programmed learning stresses impersonal, analytic skills (which suits field independents) but its non-negotiable posture makes it difficult for those who have clearly defined personal goals (such as field independents). Having made these claims, Chickering then proceeds to offer what he regards as utopian solutions:

> The solution to contract learning lies simply in employing teachers who can distinguish the field-dependent student from the independent one and vary their teaching behaviours accordingly...

> The problems presented by programmed learning
> are equally simple to solve. The answer lies in
> the direction of small modules at varying levels
> of complexity and comprehensiveness (i.e. to
> cater for choice).   (1978:87-8)

The ideal adult teacher then, is one who can
diagnose learning styles and select, from an armoury
of skills and techniques, the appropriate strategy
for enhancing learning. It is a mistake to link a
particular teaching method (such as contract
learning) to a particular cognitive style. Each
method can be implemented in a variety of ways which
may or may not match the learner's style.
Given what has been said in the preceding
discussion, the term 'diagnose' appears
inappropriate for describing the role of the adult
educator. It implies a privileged position which is
(or should be) illusory. Ideally, learning styles
should be on the agenda of any adult learning group,
not as an instrument of the adult educator, but as
an item for discussion and mutual scrutiny.

Learning styles and the experiential learning model

Kolb and Fry (1975) and Kolb (1981, 1984) have
developed an approach to classifying learning styles
which is somewhat different to that of Witkin and
his colleagues. The most important difference is
that the learning styles they identify (Table 6.2)
are closely linked to a model of the learning
process, which is represented in Figure 6.2.
In this model, learning is conceived as a four
stage cycle comprising an immediate concrete
experience, observation and reflection on that
experience, the formulation of an hypothesis or some
kind of theory, and finally the testing of that
theory through practical action. They argue that in
any learning there is a conflict or tension between
the polarities of at least two dimensions. The
first of these dimensions has the concrete
here-and-now experience at one pole, and abstract
conceptualisation at the other. The second
dimension has practical action and experimentation
at one pole and detached reflective observation at
the other. The ideal learner has the capacity to
operate at either pole of both dimensions.

> The learner, if he is to be effective, needs
> four different kinds of abilities - Concrete
> Experience abilities (CE), Reflective

Observation abilities (RO), Abstract
Conceptualisation abilities (AC) and Active
Experimentation (AE) abilities. That is, he
must be able to involve himself fully, openly
and without bias in new experiences (CE), he
must be able to reflect on and observe these
experiences from many perspectives (RO), he must
be able to create concepts that integrate his
observations into logically sound theories (AC)
and he must be able to use these theories to
make decisions and solve problems (AE).
(1975:35-6)

Figure 6.2: The experiential learning model

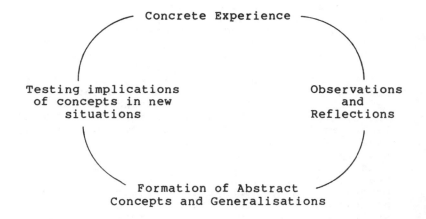

Source: Kolb and Fry, 1975:33

As it turns out, there are very few ideal learners,
and most of us develop a preference or strength in
one of the poles of each dimension. Kolb and Fry
(1976) have developed a Learning Style Inventory,
which is designed to measure a person's relative
position on the 'concrete experience' vs 'abstract
conceptualisation' dimension and the 'active
experientation' vs 'reflective observation'
dimension. The inventory consists of lists of words
which the respondent is asked to rank-order
according to how best they describe his or her
learning style. For example, if one chose the words
'analytical', 'thinking', 'logical',
'conceptualisation' and 'rational' in preference to
'receptive', 'feeling', 'accepting', 'intuitive',

101

'present-oriented' and 'experience', then a preference for abstract conceptualisation over concrete experience would be indicated. Using this procedure Kolb and Fry identified four basic learning styles, which are described in Table 6.2.

Many of the research findings, questions and issues raised in the immediately preceding section are pertinent to the learning styles described in Table 6.2. For example, there has been research linking these learning styles to vocational choices, professional socialisation, choice of undergraduate majors, preference for different teaching methods and so on. Such issues as how best to alter one's dominant style, whether to match or mis-match teaching and learning styles and how context influences one's style are relevant here in much the same way as in the discussion of field dependence/independence. To prevent repetition I will avoid any elaboration of these in the present context and instead comment on some of the unique aspects of Kolb and Fry's approach.

Like Witkin and his colleagues, Kolb and Fry challenge the notion that learning potential is reducible to a single dimension such as intelligence. Witkin showed us that there are at least two different but (ostensibly) equally valid ways of understanding the world. Similarly, Kolb and Fry argue, in opposition to received opinion, that the ability to think abstractly is no 'better' than the ability to be 'concrete'. But Kolb and Fry proceed one step further than Witkin when they acknowledge that each learning style has its strengths and weaknesses and therefore a person locked exclusively into one style is an incomplete learner. Becoming a 'complete' learner entails integrating the bi-polar dimensions of each learning style, and operating comfortably in any learning style. They then proceed to link the notion of the 'complete' learner with a model of human development whereby a long period of accentuating one's dominant learning style (because of educational experiences and vocational choices) is followed by a capacity for integration (the reason for this is not clear). This should not be taken too seriously because it is not a model which is worked out in detail and there is no evidence offered in its support. I mention it only because it illustrates another attempt to connect the 'complete learner' with a utopian conception of psychological development.

Kolb and Fry, I think, are too extravagant in the significance they attach to their 'learning

Table 6.2: Kolb and Fry's learning styles

Learning styles	Learning characteristics	Description
Converger	Abstract conceptualisation + Active experimentation	. strong in the practical application of ideas . performs well when there is a single correct answer (e.g. IQ tests) . can focus hypothetical - deductive reasoning on specific problems . unemotional, prefers to deal with things rather than people . has narrow interests and chooses to specialise in the physical sciences . characteristic of many engineers
Diverger	Concrete experience + Reflective observation	. strong in imaginative ability . good at generating ideas and seeing things from different perspectives . interested in people . broad cultural interests . specialises in arts . characteristic of people with humanities and liberal arts backgrounds
Assimilator	Abstract conceptualisation + Reflective observation	. strong ability to create theoretical models . excels in inductive reasoning . concerned with abstract concepts rather than people - not too concerned with the practical use of theories . attracted to basic sciences and mathematics . often works in research and planning departments

Table 6.2: Kolb and Fry's learning styles (cont'd)

Learning styles	Learning character- istics	Description
Accommodator	Concrete experience + Active experiment- ation	• greatest strength is in doing things • more of a risk taker • performs well when required to quickly adapt to immediate circumstances • solves problems intuitively • relies on others for information • often found in action- oriented jobs such as marketing and sales

(Adapted from Kolb and Fry, 1975)

styles'. Even though the four learning styles are neatly constructed from dimensions which correspond to a model of the learning cycle - the model is not thereby validated. Clearly the model is not generalisable to all learning environments, different learning enivornments demand different learning styles (and Kolb and Fry cite this evidence) and there is no suggestion that it should be otherwise. What is then meant by the 'complete' learner? Is it someone who can adapt his or her learning style to any learning environment or is it someone who consistently applies an 'integrated' learning strategy to all learning environments? Kolb and Fry opt for the latter interpretation where the 'complete learner':

> ... is marked by increasing complexity and relativism in dealing with the world and one's experiences and by higher level integrations of the dialectical conflicts between the four primary adaptive modes - Concrete Experience, Reflective Observation, Abstract Conceptualisation and Active Experimentation. (1975:41)

Clearly they have in mind something much more grand than simply the ability to use whatever adaptive mode is suitable for the occasion. The complete learner is able to 'integrate' the 'dialectical'

tension among the four adaptive modes - in this way
the experiential learning model becomes a model of
the complete learner.
      I find it difficult to accept this
interpretation for two basic reasons. Firstly, it
only seems to make sense in a very general, abstract
way such as when one is discussing changes in the
self and how it adapts to the world. As noted
earlier the experiential learning model does not
apply to every concrete learning situation we
encounter, that is, not every learning situation
demands a balanced integration of concrete
experience, reflective observation, abstract
conceptualisation and active experimentation.
However, most learning situations can be described
in terms of one or more of these 'adaptive modes' -
thus the experiential learning model is best
conceived as a classification scheme than as a model
of learning. Secondly, existing empirical support
for the model is weak. The Learning Style Inventory
has no capacity to measure the degree of integration
of learning styles. Indeed, it really only measures
the relative preference of one set of words over
another in describing learning styles. It is
certainly not a measure of learning style
competence; it is a measure of preference only so it
is conceivable that person 'A' as a converger will
be better at divergent thinking than person 'B' who
is a diverger. This limitation of the Learning
Style Inventory constrains the extent to which it
can be used to support the experiential learning
model.
      These objections do not preclude the possibility
of using the experiential learning model to inform
adult education practice. As a rule of thumb the
model provides an excellent framework for planning
teaching and learning activities and it can be
usefully employed as a guide for understanding
learning difficulties, vocational counselling,
academic advising and so on. But one needs to be
careful and avoid accepting the model in its
entirety because it can lead to a number of
misconceptions about learners. For example, that
everyone has a learning style which narrows their
capacity as a learner, or that some learners are
incapable of integrating their knowledge because
they are at a lower stage of psychological
development; or, finally, that there are two
'classes' of learner, the privileged class (who can
integrate their knowledge) and the less privileged
class (who are not capable of this integration).

Concluding remarks

At the close of the section on field dependence/independence I remarked that learning style information should be shared with the learners. This view is also espoused by Dixon (1985) who argues that we should abandon the 'instructor-controlled' implementation model of learning style information. Nevertheless, she does specify a role for the instructor, whose responsibilities are:

1. Helping individuals understand themselves as learners (e.g. through the critical application of learning style inventories and through introspection).
2. Encouraging individuals to expand their learning styles (e.g. by discussing learning strategies with students).
3. Using a variety of instructional approaches (so that learners experience different ways of learning).
4. Creating an environment in which diversity can thrive (e.g. through the creative use of learning contracts).
5. Creating a climate in which collaboration exists (e.g. by using others as resources).

These principles form, in my view, the best statement to date on how best to apply learning style information to adult education practices.

Chapter Seven

BEHAVIOURISM

Background

Gauging the initial reaction of people to different
psychological theories can be very instructive. For
example, psychoanalysis is often peremptorily
dismissed as an affront to commonsense knowledge, a
reaction which is typically diluted with further
exploration. By way of contrast, the vocabulary of
behaviourism (conditioning, reward, punishment,
stimulus, response) is usually received
sympathetically because it is consistent with the
casual observations we make about human behaviour.
It is only when the origin of this vocabulary is
made explicit that we baulk and reassess our
position. This chapter is the product of just such
a reassessment.

It is usual to attribute the beginning of
behaviourism to John Watson who published
'Psychology as the Behaviourist Views It' in 1913.
He argued, as did others to follow, that psychology
should be redefined as the study of behaviour and
that it should abandon the examination of
inaccessible and unobservable mental events. In
this way the scientific obligation to be 'objective'
would be fulfilled. Watson assumed that most of our
behaviour is acquired, through learning, which is to
say that it is the result of environmental rather
than biological influences. Thus the study of
learning and the conditions under which it occurs
became the core project of behaviourism. Naturally,
the type of learning which attracted the attention
of the behaviourists was the acquisition of
stereotyped responses (e.g. Pavlov's dogs salivating
when a bell rings) and the acquisition of observable
and quantifiable skills and knowledge (e.g.
recalling a list of nonsense syllables). Also, in

order to identify the environmental influences on
learning it was necessary to conduct experiments in
carefully controlled environments. The logic of
this approach ruled out investigating humans in a
natural setting, the law (or professional ethics)
ruled out investigating humans in the laboratory
setting and so the natural candidate for learning
experiments was the laboratory animal, usually the
albino rat, dog, pigeon, or rhesus monkey.

Using animals in a laboratory setting to
discover the principles of learning is a hallmark of
the behaviourist method. The most widely known
'classic' experiments are those of the Russian
physiologist Pavlov (1927), who 'conditioned' a dog
to salivate to the sound of a bell, and the American
psychologist Skinner (1938) who enticed rats and
pigeons to press or peck a lever to obtain pellets
of food in an apparatus which is now known as the
'Skinner Box'. For the present purpose, Skinner's
work will be taken as representing the behaviourist
paradigm. This is because, firstly, he embodies the
most extreme or radical form of behaviourism and,
secondly, his views have had a direct impact on
educational theory and teaching practice.

Skinner argues that organisms simply emit
responses which are gradually shaped by their
consequences. When a response (bit of behaviour)
has a rewarding (reinforcing) consequence, it is
more likely to occur again; when it has a
non-rewarding consequence, it is less likely to
occur again. In this way we acquire a repertoire of
behaviour which is literally 'shaped' by the
environment. This process is best exemplified by
considering Skinner's early experiments with animals.

A typical experiment is to place a hungry pigeon
in an isolated and sound-proof box containing a
rather prominent button which, if pecked, will
result in a food pellet being dispensed into a
tray. The pigeon is allowed to wander about
unhindered, pecking here and there as pigeons do.
In these circumstances the pigeon will eventually
peck at the button and receive a food pellet. With
each successful peck at the button, the pigeon will
be more likely to abandon its random pecking
behaviour and stand before the food tray,
alternately pecking at the button and eating the
grain. Skinner, in effect, makes a reinforcing
consequence (the food pellet) contingent upon a
certain behaviour (pecking the button) and observes
the result. In this experimental setting he has
complete control over the consequences of the

pigeon's behaviour - in his terminology, he is able
to vary the contingencies of reinforcement and
observe the resulting behaviour. By doing just
this, Skinner is able to plot the relationships
between behaviour and reinforcement, and to develop
a vocabulary expressing these relationships. Some
examples are:

1. If the apparatus is readjusted so that no food
    pellet is delivered after the button is pecked,
    the pigeon will cease pecking at the button
    (i.e. extinction will occur);
2. If the button is illuminated each time a pellet
    of food is delivered, then the pigeon will peck
    at the button when it illuminates only, and
    ceases to deliver a pellet of food. In this
    instance the illumination itself becomes
    reinforcing and is called a <u>secondary reinforcer</u>
    to distinguish it from the <u>primary reinforcer</u>
    (food pellet) which was responsible for the
    original learning;
3. If we manually control the food dispenser, we
    can deliver a pellet of food every time the
    pigeon approaches the button. By making the
    reinforcement contingent on successively closer
    approaches to the button we can 'channel' or
    'shape' the pigeon's behaviour towards the
    desired response of pecking the button. This is
    called <u>shaping</u>;
4. The pattern of reinforcement can be varied and
    its effects on learning and extinction
    observed. The pattern of reinforcement can vary
    along a continuum from 100% (every peck of the
    button is reinforced) to zero (no pecks of the
    button are reinforced). For example, the
    mechanism may be set to reinforce every 10th
    peck, or some time interval may be required
    (say, a minute) before a peck will activate the
    food dispenser. In addition, the number of
    pecks required to activate the food dispenser
    may be varied from trial to trial or even
    randomised so that no regular pattern is
    discernible. The time interval can be similarly
    varied. These are all instances of <u>partial</u>
    <u>reinforcement</u>. If partial reinforcement is
    used, learning occurs more slowly but it
    persists for longer after reinforcement is
    discontinued. In the extreme case, where
    reinforcement occurs randomly, the response
    continues indefinitely, at least until the
    experimenter rescues the pigeon from its plight

by removing it from the box altogether.

In scenarios like the above, Skinner is intent on
uncovering the empirical relationship between
reinforcement and behaviour; as such his approach is
atheoretical, and for him the study of learning ends
when one has identified the various types of
conditioning and the principles by which they
operate.
   The criticism Skinner attracts is mainly due to
his application of the technical vocabulary of the
laboratory to the broad sweep of human behaviour.
He claims that we should dispense with vague
'mentalistic' terms such as wants, needs, wishes,
ideas, will, purpose and intention and reinterpret
them in the language of reinforcement and its
contingencies. In the most readable account of the
significance of his work, '<u>Beyond Freedom and
Dignity</u>', Skinner supplies us with a sample of what
he has in mind. Here he is describing a person who
is experiencing a host of difficulties.

> ... he lacks assurance or feels insecure or is
> unsure of himself (his behaviour is weak and
> inappropriate); he is dissatisfied or
> discouraged (he is seldom reinforced and as a
> result his behaviour undergoes extinction); he
> is frustrated (extinction is accompanied by
> emotional responses); he feels uneasy or anxious
> (his behaviour frequently has unavoidable
> aversive consequences which have emotional
> effects); there is nothing he wants to do or
> enjoys doing well, he has no feeling of
> craftsmanship, no sense of leading a purposeful
> life, no sense of accomplishment (he is rarely
> reinforced for doing anything); he feels guilty
> or ashamed (he has previously been punished for
> idleness or failure, which now evokes emotional
> responses); he is disappointed in himself or
> disgusted with himself (he is no longer
> reinforced by the admiration of others, and the
> extinction which follows has emotional
> effects)...   (1973:144)

In a later section of the same publication he
asserts that the notion of a 'self' as the
originator of action is misguided and that
'identity' is reducible to a:

> ... repertoire of behaviour appropriate to a
> given set of contingencies... The picture which

emerges from a scientific analysis is not of a
body with a person inside, but of a body which
is a person in the sense that it displays a
complex repertoire of behaviour.   (1973: 194-95)

Thus, for Skinner, the scope of his work is
unlimited and there is nothing in the human
condition which can escape his analysis. If he were
less articulate or influential he may well have been
ignored, as it is, his views have provoked vehement
criticism. The two most important lines of
criticism focus on the shortcomings of his
experimental paradigm and the limited explanatory
power of his technical vocabulary.

Deficits in the experimental paradigm

Braginsky and Braginsky outline two related
objections to the type of laboratory experiment
utilised by Skinner:

> 'In this environment, behaviour is not examined
> from the point of view of the organism who is
> behaving (i.e. how it feels about what it is
> doing, or how it interprets its own behaviour)
> or from the social context in which the organism
> is interacting (i.e. the social forces that are
> present in the interaction between the
> researcher and his subject).'   (1974: 46-7)

For practical reasons alone these considerations
must be dismissed when experimenting with animals.
However, the heart of the matter is that Skinner
feels justified in making generalisations about
human beings on the basis of results obtained in the
experimental laboratory. The objection to this is
not that humans are different from animals, but that
the artificial and tightly controlled laboratory
environment is different from everyday life. An
important aspect of everyday life is that
interactions occur between people, and to make sense
of these we need to know something about the social
context in which they occur and the perceptions of
the parties concerned.
  Even Skinner, unwittingly, makes assumptions
about the context of his laboratory experiments. On
the face of it there is nothing in the Skinnerian
logic which would prevent us from reinterpreting his
observations in a perverse way (as cartoonists have
done); and construe the experimenter's behaviour as
being 'conditioned' by the pigeon pecking the disc.

But we do not do this because we perceive the experimenter to be the agent who dispenses reinforcement and controls the proceedings. Skinner's animals are always placed in a position where the consequences of their actions appear to be the result of the 'way things are' and not caused by another organism, such as the experimenter. But when an animal or human perceives an agent or person to be the cause of their pain or pleasure, then their behaviour changes quite dramatically, as Martin observes:

> If you arrange a mechanical dispenser of dog biscuits which your puppy then learns to operate, it is justifiable to claim that he is instrumentally conditioned. If, however, you invariably dispense his biscuits by hand so that you appear in the event as an agent, he will come to fawn on you in a way quite different from the way he treats the food dispenser. There is, then, a distinction to be made between conditioning in its technical sense and reward and punishment, because in the latter case the responsibility as a person or agent for the pain or pleasure enters the perception of the organism being manipulated.   (1980: 113)

Skinner is careful to avoid such loose terms as 'reward' and 'punishment' because they imply all manner of mentalistic notions having to do with agents and the perception of agency. But Martin argues, quite correctly, that the term reinforcement should be restricted in its use to describing those instances where there is no perceived agent dispensing pellets of food or whatever. It may be appropriate for the Skinner Box, but it has little generalisability beyond that context.

Explanatory power

There are three general considerations which lead us to question the explanatory power of a Skinnerian approach. First, there are a range of phenomena which appear to resist a conditioning explanation. For example, there are those instances where skills are used in a highly flexible way, as in the use of language; there are those cases where people do things which lead only to intangible rewards; and there are all those cases where people appear to learn passively, by observing others' actions rather than responding to the consequences of their own

actions. Dissatisfaction with Skinner's explanation
for each of these, but particularly the last
mentioned, resulted in a considerable reworking of
his approach among learning theorists. For example,
Bandura (1969) found it necessary to acknowledge the
importance of internal cognitive variables to
explain observational learning. Observational
learning is learning which occurs through observing
the consequences of others' behaviour. Typically
the observers gain an inkling of the pattern of
rewards and punishments which will come their way
should they imitate another's behaviour. This
brings us to the second general consideration
concerning the explanatory power of behaviourism -
whether alternative explanations can be offered for
the various 'conditioning' experiments.

Martin, for one, has constructed an alternative
explanation for the different degrees of resistance
to extinction associated with different patterns of
reinforcement. He regards the organism as a pattern
perceiver:

> 'The most easily discerned pattern of events is
> that in which reinforcement follows every peck
> at the button (I00% reinforcement). The peck
> and the delivery of grain appear as two events
> which are invariably linked in time. If we then
> shut off reinforcement completely, each
> subsequent peck at the button can be regarded as
> an experiment (on the bird's part) which has
> negative results. Under these conditions,
> extinction is rapid, and we should suggest that
> this is because each peck produces a lot of
> information about the new state of the
> environment. In extinction trials which follow
> learning under, say, 25% reinforced trials, four
> pecks could be necessary to acquire the same
> amount of information.'   (1980: 114)

This reasoning can be applied to explain the effects
on extinction of all the possible combinations of
partial reinforcement. It is an explanation which
is unacceptable to Skinner because it presupposes
that the organism guides its own behaviour according
to the patterns it discovers in the world. And yet
it is a plausible presupposition, especially given
some of the aspects of human behaviour cited
earlier, such as the capacity of humans to learn
through observing others - which may lead them to
refrain from unacceptable behaviour without
experiencing punishment or strive to gain a reward

never previously experienced. One could multiply
examples like these, but the general point is
already made that the behaviour of animals in a
'Skinner Box' can be explained without recourse to
the term 'conditioning' and that this is also true
of human behaviour in a natural setting.

A third consideration in evaluating the
explanatory power of behaviourism is the status of
its technical vocabulary. It was noted earlier that
Skinner advocates translating the vocabulary of
everyday life into the vocabulary of behaviourism.
The discourse of behaviourism appears to be sterile
and mechanistic, but it would be tolerable if it
aided our understanding. But does it? A useful
approach in answering this question is to consider
more closely a basic concept, reinforcement, and how
it is used in the principle referred to as the 'law
of conditioning', which in a paraphrased form reads:
'if the occurrence of a bit of behaviour is followed
by the presence of a reinforcing stimulus, the
strength of that behaviour is increased' (1938: 21).

But elsewhere in the same publication Skinner
defines a reinforcing stimulus by its power to
produce this change in response strength. This
definition makes the so-called 'law' a tautology.
Chomsky makes this assessment:

> The phrase 'X is reinforced by Y (stimulus,
> state of affairs, event, etc.)' is being used as
> a cover term for 'X wants Y', 'X likes Y', 'X
> wishes that Y were the case', etc. Invoking the
> term 'reinforcement' has no explanatory force,
> and any idea that this paraphrase introduces any
> new clarity or objectivity into the description
> of wishing, liking, etc. is a serious delusion.
> (1959: 38)

Other terms in the behaviourist vernacular such as
'stimulus', 'response' and 'conditioning' have been
subjected to the same type of criticism. But in
spite of this 'conditioning' is still frequently
invoked to explain human behaviour, and it is
particularly favoured among educationalists and
others with an interest in behavioural control. For
example, behaviourism continues to be associated
with innovations in the technology of teaching, such
as programmed learning and modern versions of the
'teaching machine', both of which operate in a
fashion which is analogous to the mechanical food
dispenser in a Skinnerian experiment. In adult

education its influence is most apparent in the
literature on behavioural objectives, which is the
subject of the remainder of this chapter.

Behavioural objectives

There is something very compelling in the
proposition that, at the commencement of learning,
both the teacher and learner should be clear about
the intent. A clear intent implies a goal or
objective which can be used for developing learning
activities and measuring progress and achievement.
Moreover, keeping the learner informed (or, better
still, involved in setting objectives) is surely an
open, honest and democratic thing to do. By
contrast, an authoritarian approach obscures the
intent of learning. Teachers are free to shift the
ground-rules according to their every whim and
learners are rendered impotent as they become
enmeshed in an elaborate guessing game about 'what
the teacher really wants us to learn'. Given the
above, it seems odd that some commentators have
rejected learning objectives as being incompatible
with the best traditions of adult education
(Huberman, 1974; MacDonald Ross, 1975; Robinson and
Taylor, 1983). When this rejection is apparent, it
is normally voiced about a particular type of
learning objective, the 'behavioural objective'.
    The vocabulary of behavioural objectives sits
very comfortably with the behaviourist tradition,
and it serves a similar function. This is
illustrated by the following passage from Gronlund:

> Let's try another pair of statements to be sure
> you can tell the difference between behavioural
> and non-behavioural terms. Which one of the
> following clearly indicates a behavioural
> statement?
>
> 1.   Predicts the outcome of an experiment.
> 2.   Sees the value of an experiment.
>
> This time you should have had little difficulty
> in selecting the first statement as the correct
> answer. The term 'sees' is a common one in
> education (e.g. 'I see the point'), and its
> familiarity might have misled you. But note
> that 'sees' refers to an internal state. What
> observable behaviour will the student exhibit
> when he 'sees' the value of an experiment? Will
> he describe its usefulness, point out its

> theoretical implications, or estimate the social
> consequences of the results? We simply can't
> tell because the term 'sees' is vague,
> indefinite, and describes a reaction that is not
> directly observable.   (1978: I3)

Like the behaviourist there is an emphasis on
removing from the vocabulary terms which refer to
internal states. The reason is that such terms are
not directly observable and therefore it is
impossible to tell whether learning objectives are
being achieved. The argument is that learning
outcomes can best be described in terms of changes
in the learner's behaviour. What is needed then, is
a set of guidelines for teachers and learners to
help them state their learning intent
unambiguously. The way to do this is to formulate
objectives using verbs that refer to observable
behaviour only. We cannot observe someone
'recognising' or 'knowing' something, but we can
observe them 'identifying' or 'describing' something
– so the latter terms are preferred. It is
permissible to use such vague terms as 'applies',
'comprehends', 'knows' and 'understands', but only
if they are further defined by a list of the types
of behaviour students are to demonstrate when the
objectives have been achieved. Thus:

> Place under each general instructional objective
> a list of specific learning outcomes that
> describes the terminal behaviour students are to
> demonstrate when they have achieved the
> objective.
>
> a.   Begin each specific learning outcome with a
>   verb that specifies definite, observable
>   behaviour.
> b.   List a sufficient number of specific
>   learning outcomes under each objective to
>   describe adequately the behaviour of
>   students who have achieved the objective.
> c.   Be certain that the behaviour in each
>   specific learning outcome is relevant.
>   (1978: 18)

Another point of contact with behaviourism is that
behavioural objectives are seen to be appropriate
for every conceivable type of learning. An instance
of this is when Gronlund supplies us with an
exhaustive list of illustrative verbs for stating
specific learning outcomes for 'creative

behaviours', 'drama behaviours', 'music behaviours', 'complex, logical, judgemental behaviours', 'social behaviours' and many others. Another instance can be found in Bloom's (1956) well known '<u>Taxonomy of Educational Objectives</u>', which, in its successive revisions over the years, represents an attempt to categorise all possible learning outcomes in a matrix of 'domains' and 'levels' of knowledge. It is this rather ambitious claim for the role of behavioural objectives (a claim which is echoed in training programs for adult educators) which prompts critical comment.

A reservation commonly expressed about behavioural objectives is that they fragment learning into narrowly conceived categories of behaviour which lose 'sight of the forest of skilled competence for the trees of perfected performances' (Bruner, 1971: 113). The distinction between competence and performance is important here. Even staunch advocates of behavioural objectives insist that the learning outcomes being measured should reflect the underlying competence of the learner (in this respect they differ from their behaviourist counterparts). But do behavioural objectives offer us the best method for measuring competence? There are several reasons for believing that they do not.

1. All the behavioural indicators of competence can rarely be determined in advance. People express their competence, in whatever field, in a variety of imaginative and unpredictable ways. Conversely they can be blocked from demonstrating their competence for apparently trivial reasons. For example, if we wished to measure the logical reasoning competence of a learner, we may specify a behavioural objective such as: 'To identify the validity or invalidity of a set of 'conclusions' derived from a corresponding set of premises (without error and under test conditions)'. And we may require the learner to identify the validity of the following argument:

   'If God exists, then he is everywhere.
   God is not everywhere.
   Therefore God does not exist'.

   Religious people have difficulty correctly identifying the validity of the above conclusion - not because they are incompetent at reasoning logically, but because they have a strong belief in the falsity of the conclusion. They generally perform better on syllogisms without a religious content (Feather, 1964). There are two points which can be drawn from this example. Firstly, we cannot generalise from 'behaviour' to 'competence' without taking into account the context in which the behaviour occurs, and it is impossible to control or predict every aspect of the context (e.g. learner's motivation, past experience, variables associated with the testing situation). Secondly, because the context is largely unpredictable, we should not limit ourselves to pre-planned conceptions of what is, and what is not, a fair behavioural indicator of competence.

2. The emphasis on terminal learning outcomes undervalues the importance of the learning process. The preoccupation with the end point of instruction is mitigated somewhat by what are called 'enabling' objectives, which refer to assessable marker points along the learning path. The difficulty with this is that people learn at different rates and have different styles of learning, so any pre-determined, uniform monitoring of progress is likely to favour some and hinder others. It is not simply that these tests are unfair, but that, because of their focus on observable behaviour, they do an injustice to the complexity of learning. For example, in mastering a complex skill, such as playing the piano, learning can proceed along a multitude of dimensions - posture, finger position, notation, use of the pedal, scale drill, chord progressions, and so on. However, not all these dimensions can be separated for instructional purposes - even if this were the case it would be wrong to measure progress along each separate dimension as an indicator of progress towards the ultimate objective. This is because what is most important in learning complex skills is how the various dimensions 'come together' to form an integrated whole. And it is precisely this type of outcome which resists behavioural analysis. It becomes necessary to employ so called 'imprecise' and 'vague' terms to assist learning and measure progress.

3. Not all learning outcomes are specifiable in behavioural terms.

Bruner, in his classic essay on 'The Process of Education', outlines two ways in which learning can serve us in the future.

> One is through its specific applicability to tasks that are highly similar to those we originally learned to perform. Psychologists refer to this phenomenon as specific transfer of training; perhaps it should be called the extension of habits or associations. Its utility appears to be limited in the main to what we usually speak of as skills. Having learned how to hammer nails, we are better able later to learn how to hammer tacks or chip wood. Learning in school undoubtedly creates skills of a kind that transfer to activities encountered later, either in school or after. A second way in which earlier learning renders later performance more efficient is through what is conveniently called non-specific transfer or, more accurately, the transfer of principles and attitudes. In essence, it consists of learning initially not a skill but a general idea, which can then be used as a basis for recognizing subsequent problems as special cases of the idea originally mastered.   (1966: 17)

Behavioural objectives, because they relate only to the specific observable outcomes of learning, cannot address adequately the acquisition of the basic and general ideas referred to above.

This is because these ideas can only have meaning in terms of a general and abstract level of discourse. For example, a valued learning outcome among industrial trainers is 'safety consciousness'. But what is meant by this? Can we reduce it to a specific set of performance indicators such as 'describes the procedure to be followed in an emergency' or 'lists the safety rules of the workshop'? I doubt it - no matter how exhaustive and valuable our list of performance indicators they can never collectively capture the spirit of 'safety consciousness'. We must make recourse to terms like 'values', 'appreciates', 'feels', or 'understands' in order to give expression to what we mean by 'safety consciousness'. True, we can only assess it by observing people's behaviour, but we cannot specify what this behaviour will be - beyond describing, in abstract terms, the principles to which the behaviour must conform.

Another line of argument is that objectives, almost by definition, cannot be derived for subjective outcomes like 'development of self concept' (Robinson and Taylor, 1983). What are the performance indicators of an improved self concept? Our judgements about such things are derived from a complex array of observations, their connections and the inferences we make from them. We could attempt to operationalise the concept but this would require us to select a few key performance indicators from an infinite variety of possible observations. Such an exercise would be artificial and futile, and it would do an injustice to the complexity of what we mean by 'self concept'.

4. Learning may be occurring which is not being measured. In many respects behavioural objectives constrain our assessment of the benefits of any learning effort. The implication is that if we fail to achieve our objectives, the learning effort is wasted. Or, alternatively, that the objectives we achieve are the most important outcomes of the learning effort. Neither of these statements acknowledge the importance of unplanned or incidental learning. No teacher, or learner for that matter, has complete control over what is being learnt. Valuable learning can, and often does, occur which is outside the original intent. This type of learning should be acknowledged when evaluating any learning experience - but it is typically overlooked when behavioural objectives are used as a benchmark for success.

Robinson and Taylor (1983) draw attention to the way in which behavioural objectives imply a rational planning model of learning. This model is well exemplified by Davis et al who describe the steps in designing any learning system (see Table 7.1).

According to the above, learning can, and should, proceed in a logical and orderly manner. Robinson and Taylor (1983) argue that this type of approach is incompatible with the ethos of adult education for a number of reasons:

Table 7.1: The learning system design process

---

1. Describe current system.
2. Derive and write objectives.
3. Describe tasks.
4. Analyse tasks and objectives.
5. Plan evaluation.
6. Design instruction.
7. Implement instruction.
8. Conduct evaluation.

(Adapted from Davis et al, 1974: 19)

1. No account is taken of the unpredictability of student-centred learning, which is characterised by a constant re-definition of goals while exploring learning possibilities.
2. When learners are required to derive their own objectives there is an assumption that they know precisely what and how they want to learn, and that they can articulate their intent.
3. When objectives are specified for the learner they serve as an instrument of institutional control and they support dependency among learners.
4. Objectives function as an authoritarian support for the teacher in the sense that they are part of a controlled learning process where failure can only be the result of the learner's failings.
5. A behavioural objective is an educational tool which helps legitimise the professional nature of adult education. It is closely associated with the culture of accountability, payment by results, cost effectiveness and the 'guaranteed product' of student performance.

The above points certainly establish that behavioural objectives, as a component of the rational model of learning, have a case to answer. The rational model does indeed appear to be opposed to a 'participatory', 'democratic' and 'liberatory' adult education. But it should be said that Robinson and Taylor's comments are directed at a consistently rigorous application of the behavioural objectives approach. The same can be said of the preceding comments in this section. Robinson and Taylor deny the possibility that practitioners can use objectives as guides only - and that they can be modified, challenged, reworked or even abandoned in the pursuit of learning. 'You cannot have a 'more or less' model; its credibility depends on an internal consistency, on an internal logic. Put simply, the programme is an objective model or it isn't.' (1983: 358). Ironically, this is the type of rigid demand they profess to criticise in the rational model of learning. By allowing no scope for a flexible and tentative application of objectives, the critics seal their case. This is a legitimate thing to do, but there is always the danger of assuming that what is 'logically' necessary, is necessary in practice. In practice, behavioural objectives applied in a certain way <u>may</u> be entirely consistent with what we judge to be <u>good</u> adult education practice. The foregoing arguments simply indicate the improbability of this occurring, especially when practice rigidly follows the guidelines in the literature currently available.

Chapter Eight

GROUP DYNAMICS AND THE GROUP FACILITATOR

Group dynamics, as a field of enquiry within social psychology, is said to occupy the 'middle ground' between the person and society. This is because it is the small group which becomes the unit of analysis, the crucible, so to speak, which reveals the secrets of how the person forms, and is formed by, the social environment. A basic premise in group dynamics is that a group is more than a mere collection of individuals, that is, groups have their own dynamic quite independent of the individuals comprising them. Many theoretical perspectives and research techniques have been applied to the study of groups. It comes as no surprise to find that the various approaches to understanding group phenomena and the explanations advanced are as diverse within the field of group dynamics as they are in psychology generally. However, I wish to avoid a lengthy exposition of these different perspectives which would, in any case, require a repetition of much of what has already been said. For this reason the approach adopted in this chapter will be to explore the significance of groups for adult educators, and the way in which group dynamic concepts have (or could) be used as a foundation for practice.

The individual and the group in adult education

In contemporary adult education there is a tension between the ethic of individualism and the spirit of collectivism. Individualism is most apparent in the humanistic approach. This was touched upon earlier but is worth expanding here. The core ideas of the ethic of individualism are described by Lukes. Firstly, there 'is the ultimate moral principle of the supreme and intrinsic value, or dignity of the

individual human being' (1973:45). This constitutes a moral axiom which places the individual at the centre of a value system which relegates the 'group' to second place. Secondly, there is 'the notion of autonomy, or self-direction, according to which an individual's thought and action is his own, and not determined by agencies or causes outside his control' (1973:52). And finally, there is the notion of self-development which is steeped in the romantic tradition and which 'specifies an ideal for the lives of individuals – an ideal whose content varies with different ideas of the self on a continuum from pure egoism to strong communitarianism. It is either anti-social, with the individual set apart from and hostile to society, or extra-social, when the individual pursues his own path, free of social pressures, or highly social, where the individual's self-development is achieved through community with others' (1973:71). These three features of individualism: the dignity of the person, autonomy and self direction, and self-development, underly the value system implicit in humanistic adult education. Ironically, this value system is widespread among adult educators who nevertheless profess an understanding of groups and a commitment to group work. Symptomatic of this 'individualist' approach to groups is a conception of group work as a means to an end. The claim is that group learning is better than, say, the lecture format, because it encourages the pooling of resources, builds a sense of group belonging, allows participants to express their views, helps them to clarify their thinking, and so on. The adult educator's task is to develop an armoury of group teaching techniques, a sensitivity to the pitfalls of group work, and an ability to intervene appropriately in the group process. The ultimate aim is to establish a smoothly functioning, cohesive group in which individuals can work together and learn productively. The group dynamics literature offers an abundance of supportive material on conformity, group cohesion, leadership, communication structures, the emergence of norms, group development, group decision making, and individual versus group performance – all of which can be used in the service of understanding how the individual is influenced by the group or how a particular individual (the facilitator) can influence the life of the group.
     The collectivist spirit is best exemplified in

the writings of 'radical' adult educators such as
Freire (1972), Lovett (1983), Gelpi (1979) and
Griffin (1983). They are interested in how adult
education can contribute to radical social change
and how it can foster collective, as opposed to
individual advancement. Historical precedents often
cited as models of collective adult education are
the Highlander Folk School in Tennessee, the
Antigonish movement in Nova Scotia, the Labour
Colleges in the USA, the Scandinavian Study Circles
and the Danish co-operatives. The collectivist
spirit is overtly political in the sense that it
advocates the empowerment of certain groups in
society, such as the working class, peasants, women;
and racial, indigenous or religious minorities. It
is also opposed to adult education initiatives which
are solely used as vehicles for personal
advancement, which, in the final analysis, will only
produce 'clever rogues'. This commitment to the
group originates from a political ideology which
emphasises the importance of democratic leadership,
participation in decision making, co-operative
activities and self management. The foundations for
practice here are political and social theory,
rather than social psychology or group dynamics.
The idea of group self determination is a political
and moral imperative and the purpose of group work
is not so much to promote group cohesion or arrive
at some kind of consensus, as to provide a forum for
democratic discussion and decision making.

These two approaches to the group, the
'individualistic' and the 'collective' are best
conceived as opposite ends of a continuum along
which real life adult educators may be positioned.
The literature on group dynamics is, on balance,
more easily identified with the 'individualistic'
pole of this continuum. It corresponds to what
Olmsted and Hare refer to as the 'internal' approach
to groups:

> The second approach to the study of groups may
> be referred to as the 'internal' focus on groups
> as societies. This is a newer, experimentally
> minded tradition and derives from psychology
> more than from sociology. Groups are conceived
> of as worth studying because they are relevant
> environments for individual behaviour – they are
> the subsocieties in which social interaction and
> the individual's part in it can be observed and
> tested.   (1978:9)

This 'internal' approach to the group (as opposed to the 'external' approach, which is concerned with how groups function in larger social entities) has yielded a mass of research data and a diverse range of theoretical explanations. There now exist a number of standard 'classic' texts which provide a relatively coherent picture of the field (e.g. Cartwright and Zander, 1968; Hare, 1976; Shaw, 1981) and there are some texts specifically relating group dynamics to adult learning (e.g. McLeish, Matheson and Park, 1973; Cooper (ed), 1975; Jaques, 1984).

The interest of adult educators in group dynamics stems from a belief that it is through group learning that many of the precepts in adult education can be realised. Groups are said to promote self understanding through shared support and mutual feedback. They generate the experiential base for learning, they encourage interaction, self determination and trust. It is the group that challenges the traditional relationship between the teacher and the taught and insists on equal input into planning. Ultimately, it is only through the group that 'learning how to learn' can be achieved. Given these beliefs, the primacy given to group dynamics in the training of adult educators is understandable, even though only a brief acquaintance with the literature will reveal that each of these beliefs can be challenged.

Adult learning texts, when they refer to group dynamics, tend to select material which will assist the adult educator to:

1. Observe groups. (e.g. Bales' Interaction Process Analysis, Moreno's Sociometry technique).
2. Interpret their observations. (e.g. as a phase of group development, an instance of group influence, an indication of role differentiation, etc.).
3. Intervene in the group process. (e.g. Heron's Six Category Intervention Analysis, the myriad of group teaching techniques, the Nominal Group Technique).

The remainder of this chapter will focus on the last of the above purposes and consider some common group facilitation techniques and the more general questions they raise.

Group influence and experiential techniques

There is a tradition of research in group dynamics

which documents the powerful influence of the group on individual actions, perceptions, judgements and beliefs. There are some landmark studies in this literature and it is worth reviewing a sample of them briefly prior to discussing the nature of the experiential group.

The classic experiment in this tradition was conducted by Sherif (1935). Subjects are seated in a darkened room and required to track the apparent movement of a spot of light. The light is in fact stationary and its apparent movement is an optical illusion known as the autokinetic effect (a small stationary spot of light in a dark room normally appears to move between 50mm–150mm). When alone, individuals gradually establish a range (say 75mm–125mm) and a norm (say, 100mm) for their judgements. When people who have established such ranges and norms are brought together in groups, their ranges and norms converge into a group norm. It is the group norm which persists when subjects are asked to once again judge individually. The significance of this experiment is that it is the group norm which has a more binding force than individual norms.

A later, but equally celebrated set of studies are reported by Asch (1956). In his experiments subjects are asked to judge which of three vertical lines (of 15.5cms, 20cms and 17cms) is equivalent in length to a standard vertical line of 20cms. Subjects can perform this task with 100% accuracy when judging alone. However, when the judgement occurs in a group where the other members unanimously give an incorrect judgement (because they are confederates of the experimenter), approximately one third of the subjects go against their own senses and conform to the majority judgement for at least half the trials. This level of conformity is strikingly reduced when the subject has an 'ally' who disagrees with the majority judgement and insists on judging correctly. No satisfactory explanation for the level of yielding has been advanced to date. At the time Asch suggested that three types of yielding were apparent:

1. Those whose perceptions were actually distorted and therefore perceived the majority estimates as correct.
2. Those who accepted the correctness of the group judgement but realised that they perceived something different.
3. Those who believed their judgement to be correct

but went along with the majority decision to avoid appearing different.

These distinctions correspond to attempts made elsewhere to classify processes of group influence; such as internalisation, where the individual takes on the values of the group; identification, where the individual desires to be like the group; and compliance, where the individual 'obeys' the group norms to avoid rejection (Douglas, 1983). Despite the limitations of these earlier studies (e.g. that the groups being studied were really not 'groups' in the proper sense) they nevertheless remain powerful demonstrations of group influence.

Deception is a key research technique for many of the studies on group influence. One researcher who employed deception to an extreme (and some say 'unethical') degree was Milgram (1965). He was interested in the conditions under which people would or would not carry out another's command. The essential elements of the study are described by Milgram:

> The focus of the study concerns the amount of electric shock a subject is willing to administer to another person when ordered by an experimenter to give the 'victim' increasingly more severe punishment. The act of administering shock is set in the context of a learning experiment, ostensibly designed to study the effect of punishment on memory. Aside from the experimenter, one naive subject and one accomplice perform in each session. On arrival each subject is paid $4.50. After a general talk by the experimenter, telling how little scientists know about the effect of punishment on memory, subjects are informed that one member of the pair will serve as teacher and one as a learner. A rigged drawing is held so that the naive subject is always the teacher, and the accomplice becomes the learner. The learner is taken to an adjacent room and strapped into an 'electric chair'.

> The naive subject is told that it is his task to teach the learner a list of paired associates, to test him on the list, and to administer punishment whenever the learner errs in the test. Punishment takes the form of electric shock, delivered to the learner by means of a shock generator controlled by the naive

subject. The teacher is instructed to increase
the intensity of electric shock one step on the
generator on each error. The learner, according
to plan, provides many wrong answers, so that
before long the naive subject must give him the
strongest shock on the generator. Increases in
shock level are met by increasingly insistent
demands from the learner that the experiment be
stopped because of the growing discomfort to him
[the deception is that the 'learner' in fact
receives no shocks at all]. The responses of
the victim are standardized on tape, and each
protest is co-ordinated to a particular voltage
level on the shock generator. Starting with 75
volts the learner begins to grunt and moan. At
150 volts he demands to be let out of the
experiment. At 180 volts he cries out that he
can no longer stand the pain. At 300 volts he
refuses to provide any more answers to the
memory test, insisting that he is no longer a
participant in the experiment and must be
freed. In response to his last tactic, the
experimenter instructs the naive subject to
treat the absence of an answer as equivalent to
a wrong answer, and to follow the usual shock
procedure. The experimenter reinforces his
demand with the statement: 'You have no other
choice, you must go on!' (This imperative is
used whenever the naive subject tries to break
off the experiment). If the subject refuses to
give the next higher level of shock, the
experiment is considered at an end.   (1965:
59-60)

Using this procedure Milgram reports that over sixty
percent of subjects continue to administer the
shocks, obediently, (although with considerable
discomfort and some degree of protest) until
instructed to stop by the experimenter. The most
striking feature of this experiment (apart from
Milgram's apparent disregard for the suffering of
the naive subjects) is the high proportion of people
willing to carry out the experimenter's
instructions, even though they believe their actions
are causing considerable pain to another person.
Variations on the basic design of the experiment
reveal that obedience decreases as the physical
proximity of the learner (who is receiving the
shocks) increases and as the physical proximity of
the experimenter (who is giving the orders to
continue) decreases. From the point of view of

group influence, the most significant variation on
the basic design involves the use of groups. When
Milgram arranged for a group of disobedient cohorts
to defy the experimenter's authority in the presence
of the subjects, then 90% of the subjects followed
suit and also defied the experimenter (a group of
obedient cohorts increased the subjects' obedience
only slightly).

One last experiment looks at the effect of group
decisions about an agreed course of action on the
subsequent actions of its members. During the
Second World War the American government wished to
change the eating habits of its population towards
the consumption of poultry and meat offal. Lewin
(1958), arguing that norms emerge at a group level,
suggested trying to change eating habits through
group discussion. He then sought to demonstrate the
effectiveness of group discussion by comparing it
with the effects obtained through using lectures.
One group of subjects (all subjects were described
as Red Cross volunteer housewives) were treated to a
well prepared lecture on the desirability of diet
change and how to prepare recipes which were
attractive. A second group of subjects were allowed
to discuss the relevance of domestic diet to the war
effort, they exchanged ideas and opinions about
offal and took a vote on whether they would
experiment with a new diet. Interviews carried out
a week later show clearly the effectiveness of group
discussion: 32% of the group discussion members had
actually served one of the recommended meals, this
compares with only 3% of the subjects who received a
lecture on the subject.

From each of the four experiments mentioned
above, one can trace a line of research activity and
debate which is still in progress. Like so many
social psychological experiments they function very
much like parables. They are now enshrined in the
history of social psychology, and are used as a
reminder of how individual choice and independent
action are shaped and constrained by groups.

Thus we return to an earlier theme relating to
whose interests are served by working and learning
in groups. Group facilitators in adult education
often refer to the desirability of group
cohesiveness - which normally means the extent to
which group members are attracted to the group. The
positive consequences of group cohesiveness are well
documented for experimental, learning and working
groups and group cohesion is often portrayed as an
important step in the growth of groups towards

maturity. Given this, it is understandable that
group exercises have emerged which have as their
primary goal the enhancement of group cohesiveness.
Given also that cohesiveness is expressed in terms
of the affective, non-instrumental behaviour of the
group, it is easy to see why such group exercises
focus on the release of emotional tension, the
breakdown of defences against learning, the
enhancement of interaction among group members and
so on. The value of working towards such goals is
unquestionable. However, some of the exercises and
techniques recommended in training manuals and
practised in countless training and adult education
workshops are of questionable value. The 'ice
breaker' for example, is a familiar experience for
most people involved in adult education. Like many
experiential group techniques in adult education,
its origins can be traced to the human potential
movement and the techniques associated with it, such
as 'T-groups' and 'encounter' groups. Some of the
excesses of this movement have been documented by
Malcolm (1975), who notes three key features of the
exercises commonly used:

1. A focus on the immediate 'here-and-now'
   experience of participants.
2. A belief that individual change occurs more
   readily in groups.
3. A belief in the value of open, honest feedback
   and self disclosure.

Malcolm's objection to these (exclusively)
experiential exercises is that the individual, far
from being enhanced, must surrender to the group
will. In the typical T-group, which is an
unstructured, essentially leaderless group which has
as its purpose a fuller understanding of self and
others, the rules governing the behaviour of
participants are well known beforehand (despite
disclaimers to the contrary). On Malcolm's account
these rules operate very much against the
individual. For example, the need to focus on the
'here and now' typically appears as an aggressive
anti-intellectual attitude in the group, where the
display of individual knowledge and expertise is
invariably interpreted as a defence against the
spontaneous expression of feelings. Those
behaviours which are encouraged are those which are
prohibited in the course of normal social
interaction, at least in the adult population.
Failure to accept 'honest' and 'open' feedback

(which might mean some kind of abuse from another group member) is considered deviant, as is the failure to 'confess' one's true feelings, or worse still - not agreeing to participate in the activities of the group.

Malcolm makes a compelling case that the extreme elements of the human potential movement use techniques which are manipulative, demeaning and because they are effective, quite dangerous. His case can also be applied to some experiential techniques adopted by adult educators, particularly those used as short-cuts to establishing group cohesiveness such as the 'icebreaker'. The typical icebreaker has all the ingredients of the human potential 'experiential' exercise - it often involves some kind of childish game, it invariably requires group interaction on an emotional level, and it demands some kind of self disclosure. The following is one of 21 icebreakers recommended in 'More Games Trainers Play' by Edward Scannell and John Newstrom; it is called the 'Magic Circle':

> Divide the group into teams of five-seven people. If possible, arrange the chairs in a circular fashion. On a prepared set of 3" x 5" cards, a series of words or phrases are written (one on each card, e.g. motivation; put-down; I feel good when...). The group leader pulls a card at random and each person is asked to state what the word means to them, or in the case of sentence completion, continue the statement. Continue for five-seven minutes for each card. (1983:19)

This exercise amounts to a public display of free association among the members of the group who are meeting, presumably, for the first time. The discussion question recommended is : 'what barriers to communication did the exercise show?' The progress of this exercise would very much depend on how it was introduced and the 'climate setting' of the leader prior to introducing it. However, it is a risky exercise, and one can imagine all manner of disastrous outcomes. One option for participants is to treat the exercise in a lighthearted fashion and play along with the game of 'confessing' one's barriers to communication. But the more likely scenario here is that participants will play the game according to different rules and those who choose to take it seriously (with genuine self disclosure) will be at risk.

For the most part icebreakers are harmless games which, at the very worst, may be a little insulting to the participant's intelligence or capacity for social intercourse. But one should nevertheless be conscious of the dangers of using such exercises at the beginning of the group life. The individual at this point is likely to be more compliant and it is particularly difficult to opt for non-participation. There are, however, three fundamental principles in using group experiential techniques, which, if properly adhered to, will reduce the possibility of a harmful group experience and enhance the possibility of learning. These are:

1. The principle of informed consent i.e. the participants should be told <u>precisely</u> the nature of the exercise.
2. The principle of freedom to participate i.e. participants should be free to leave the group at any time. Ideally this freedom means freedom from the group pressure to conform, which of course is something extremely difficult to eliminate. It is therefore a principle which needs to be strongly stated and frequently reiterated by the group facilitator.
3. The principle of critical reflection, i.e. making sense of the experience by analysing and evaluating it (see Boud, et al, 1985, Zeichner and Liston, 1987).

Earlier I argued that a great deal of group work in adult education is done in the name of individual growth and development. Paradoxically, one of the greatest dangers of group work comes from the power of the group to shape and maintain the behaviour and beliefs of its members. In this context a knowledge of group dynamics can best be used to ward off oppressive aspects of the group. This is a particularly important function for adult educators who constantly witness the transformation of collections of individuals into groups of one sort or another.

Meeting the needs of the group

Groups are often seen as vehicles for enhancing learner participation in program planning - the belief is that it is only through group methods that the true needs of the group can be expressed. The idea of meeting needs, however, is not as straightforward as it initially sounds. There are those who reject the needs meeting paradigm as a legitimate approach to adult education provision (e.g. Armstrong, 1982; Griffin, 1983) claiming that it is no more than a slogan which only serves the interests of the professional providers. These commentators generally focus on the ideological workings of the needs concept and how it influences the broad sweep of adult education provision. But our concern here is with what 'needs meeting' means for an adult educator who is confronted with a group of learners and who has some notion that meeting their needs might be a good idea. The first difficulty this person will face is to distinguish between the needs, demands and wants of the group (see Wiltshire, 1973, Lawson, 1975; Tennant, 1985b). Wants are normally considered to be desires, pure and simple, without any appraisal of the value of satisfying those desires. A demand is conceived as the overt expression of a want 'we would like to learn some fundamental theorems' or 'we want more time allocated to class discussion', are examples of direct demands. An indirect demand would be the number of people who drop out of the course; as Newman has remarked: 'Having no one turn up concentrates the adult educator's mind wonderfully,' (1979:147). A need then is a 'want' or 'demand' which is deemed worthy of satisfying. Thus needs are not neutral – they require a judgement by someone about the relative merits of satisfying different wants or demands. Exactly how this judgement is to be made in a learning group is indeed problematic.

This scenario is further complicated by the contradiction of trying to meet both individual and group needs simultaneously. To assume that group needs are compatible with the interests of individual members presupposes a consensus which is rarely evident. Indeed, there is a necessary gap between the needs and interests of the group and the needs and interests of the individual. Every group at some stage infringes on individual autonomy and therefore a judgement must be made about a just or equitable arrangement for meeting the needs of the individual in the context of the group's needs.

One technique, the Nominal Group Technique (NGT) is arguably a good way to approach the two tasks of evaluating wants/demands and blending individual and group needs. The steps in this technique are outlined in Table 8.1.

This technique has been designed to allow a balanced input from all group members, especially

Table 8.1: Steps in the nominal group technique

---

1. The task is stated (e.g. what issues should this series of seminars address?).
2. Participants write down their ideas silently and independently.
3. All ideas are listed in 'round-robin' fashion with clarifying comments/questions but no discussion.
4. Ideas are defended by the proposer and agreements or disagreements are voiced.
5. Group members evaluate the ideas, list their top 5 priorities and then rank these priorities from highest (5 points) to lowest (1 point).
6. The vote is tallied and the results recorded on a flowchart.
7. Further discussion of the ideas and the voting pattern.
8. Repeat the voting process, tally the ideas and list them in rank order.

---

during the initial stages. It also preserves the anonymity of the voter thereby (presumably) reducing the pressure on the individual to conform to majority opinion. But it is a mechanical process which really only delays the issue at stake - what to do with the final list of ideas. Is the final list of ideas binding on all members of the group? Is it subject to revision? What are the conditions under which it can be revised? These questions indicate that in the NGT, the neutrality of the seminar leader and the diminution of the group dynamics process are short lived. Sooner or later the group must start functioning as a group and not as a mechanical device for meeting needs or decision making.

There are many other techniques comparable to the NGT but they mostly amount to a set of rules for decision making or problem solving which function in a similar manner to 'standing orders' in a committee meeting. But this is rarely the most fruitful way to proceed in establishing group needs. The idea that a group 'need' is there at the start of a learning process is a mistaken one. Most adult learning groups are artificial in the sense that it is individuals who come to learn and the group only emerges when there is a recognition of interdependence. Using a mechanical technique at the outset as a method of program planning will result only in an aggregation of individual needs – it will almost certainly fail to register the needs arising from the emerging interdependence within the group.

Group Development

The brief examples of group techniques in this chapter could be multiplied. The point I wish to draw from them is that groups are not mechanical objects which can be manipulated by a skilled facilitator.

The literature on group development confirms this view. In general it considers groups to be organic entities with characteristic and predictable patterns of growth and development. Jaques (Table 8.2) summarises and tabulates ten well-known approaches to describing group development. An inspection of this table reveals that they all identify between three and six 'stages' or 'phases' in group life, which are typically described in terms of how the group sorts out its authority, power and interpersonal relationships. Tuckman's (1965) analysis portrays in a simple manner the principal features of this literature. He describes groups as moving through the following stages:

1. Forming – where there is anxiety, dependence on a leader, and testing to find out the nature of the situation and what behaviour is acceptable.
2. Storming – where there is a conflict between sub-groups, rebellion against the leader, a polarisation of opinions, and emotional resistance to the demands of the task.
3. Norming – where norms emerge and there is a development of an open exchange of views and feelings.
4. Performing – where interpersonal problems are resolved and there are constructive attempts to complete the task.

This development process has much in common with the lifespan developmental theories discussed earlier – there is a linear, step-by-step progression from immaturity to maturity which occurs across a range of group types (natural groups, laboratory groups, training groups, therapy groups etc.). Some approaches extend the parallel with individual lifespan development one step further and include the decline and death of the group (e.g.

Table 8.2: Some approaches to group development

		Phase I: Dependence		Phase II: Interdependence		
Thelen and Dickerman (1949)	PHASE 1: Individually centred	PHASE 2: Frustration and conflict	PHASE 3: Attempted consolidation of group harmony	PHASE 4: Individual self-assessment, flexibility of group process, emphasis upon productivity in problem solving.		
Miles (1953)	PHASE 1: Unoriented, restive "talking about" irrelevant matters	PHASE 2: Abstract "talking about" leadership and permissiveness	PHASE 3: "Doing level" – Discussion and analysis of here-and-now			
Bennis & Shepard (1956)	SUBPHASE 1: Dependence-submission	SUBPHASE 2: Counter-dependence	SUBPHASE 3: Resolution	SUBPHASE 4: Enchantment	SUBPHASE 5: Disenchantment	SUBPHASE 6: Conceptual validation
Schutz (1955)	PHASE 1: Inclusion	PHASE 2: Control	PHASE 3: Affection			
Bion (1968)	STAGE 1: Flight	STAGE 2: Fight	STAGE 3: Unite			
Bradford (1964)	STAGE 1: Ambiguity	STAGE 2: Self-investment participation	STAGE 3: Collaboration and learning from peers	STAGE 4: Motivation for learning	STAGE 5: Experienced behaviour and feedback	STAGE 6: Group growth and development
Mills (1964)	STAGE 1: The encounter	STAGE 2: Testing boundaries and modelling behaviour	STAGE 3: Negotiating and indigenous normative system	STAGE 4: Production	STAGE 5: Separation	
Tuckman (1965)	STAGE 1: Forming– Testing and dependence	STAGE 2: Storming– Intragroup conflict	STAGE 3: Norming– Development of group cohesion	STAGE 4: Performing– Functional role relatedness		
Mann (1967)	PHASE 1: Initial complaining	PHASE 2: Premature enactment	PHASE 3: Confrontation	PHASE 4: Internalization		
Dunphy (1968)	PHASE 1: Maintenance of external normative standard	PHASE 2: Individual rivalry and aggression	PHASE 3: Realization of unattainable utopian ideals		PHASES 5 and 6: Separation and terminal review	End of group

Source: Jaques, 1984:34

Mills, 1964; Mann, 1967; and Dunphy, 1968). Others minimise the linear-progressive aspects of group development and emphasise instead the recurring nature of the 'phases' or 'stages' of group life, (e.g. Bion, 1968, Schutz, 1955).

Most adult educators who work with groups have a sense of the evolution of group identity and the fluctuations in group life which accompany this process. The group development literature is useful in that it helps the adult educator to interpret events occurring within the group. However it is unclear how the adult educator should respond to these events and intervene in the group process. The option most frequently discussed in the literature is to devise strategies for facilitating the group through its various phases. In this role the adult educator operates rather like a lubricant in a motor car - it ensures a smoothly functioning process but has no regard for direction and destination. This role is appropriate only where the group is genuinely free to pursue its own course - but this is rarely the case and most adult learning groups function within non-negotiable parameters and constraints. A fatal mistake in organising any adult learning group is to create an illusion of freedom in the group which in fact does not exist. For example an orientation program for a group of adult learners may be organised around their perceptions of what they want to learn and how they intend to accomplish their goals. The organisers may have designed the orientation to facilitate the process of group development. They may be putting into practice Bennis and Shephard's (1956) recommendation that at the first stage of group development the organiser should abnegate the traditional role of structuring the situation, setting up the rules of play and so on. When this illusion of freedom is shattered and the external constraints are made explicit the organisers may interpret the subsequent hostility of the group towards them as simply indicating the next phase of group development (disenthrallment with organisers). However this would be trivialising what would be more accurately interpreted as a predictable response to being deceived.

The point emerging from the above hypothetical scenario is that group events need to be interpreted in terms of the context in which the group exists. Groups do not operate in a vacuum with their own internal logic and developmental timetable. The dynamics of a group reflect not only its level of maturity, but the external constraints operating on it. A change in these external constraints can have an effect on group dynamics which overrides any ongoing developmental process. To this extent any notion of group maturity is at best provisional.

To conclude, much of the applied group dynamics literature places too much emphasis on the skills of the group facilitator and too little emphasis on how a knowledge of group dynamics can be used to empower the group. Notwithstanding this, most adult educators would acknowledge the importance of building a good climate for learning and fostering connections among the students. This may require a temporary suspension of critical thought and analysis whilst the group explores their feelings and expresses their concerns. It is at these moments that the group facilitator thrives - as a director of the process, but not the content. A highly cohesive and consensual group however, should never be seen as an end in itself - there are always the broader questions to be considered such as 'cohesion for what purpose?' and 'cohesion at what price?' - questions which are often overlooked by that skilled adult learning technician, the group facilitator.

Chapter Nine

CRITICAL AWARENESS

Myles Horton, the radical baptist minister who
established the Highlander Folk School in Tennessee
in the 1930s, once remarked 'An unanalysed
experience is a kind of a happening' (Horton,
1986). When he made this remark he was leading a
seminar on his work at Highlander and he was being
questioned about his approach to teaching and
learning. He observed that the people with whom he
worked - the poor, blacks, labour groups - had never
been encouraged to analyse their experiences. His
approach was to build programs based on real
problems, help groups analyse their collective
experiences of those problems and encourage some
form of collective action to bring about social
change (see Adams, 1975). The idea of analysing
one's experiences to achieve liberation from
psychological repression (e.g. psychoanalysis) or
social and political oppression is a recurring theme
in adult education. It is most commonly identified
with the work of Freire (1972, 1974) but it is also
a feature of some comtemporary conceptions of
self-directed learning (Brookfield, 1985a) andragogy
(Mezirow, 1983) action research (Carr and Kemmis
1983, Kemmis, 1985) models of the learning process
(Jarvis, 1987a, 1987b) and techniques of
facilitation (Boud et al, 1985, 1987).
     Freire (1974) adopts the term 'conscientisation'
to describe the process whereby people come to
understand that their view of the world and their
place in it (their consciousness) is shaped by
social and historical forces which work against
their own interests. 'Conscientisation' leads to a
critical awareness of the self as a subject who can
reflect and act upon the world in order to transform
it. Freire applied his ideas while working with
literacy programs in Brazil in the early 1960s:

From the beginning, we rejected the hypothesis
of a purely mechanistic literacy program and
considered the problem of teaching adults how to
read in relation to the awakening of their
consciousness. We wished to design a project in
which we would attempt to move from naivety to a
critical attitude at the same time we taught
reading. We wanted a literacy program which
would be an introduction to the democratization
of culture, a program with men as its subjects
rather than as patient recipients,... The more
accurately men grasp true causality, the more
critical their understanding of reality will
be. Their understanding will be magical to the
degree that they fail to grasp causality.
Further, critical consciousness always submits
that causality to analysis; what is true today
may not be so tomorrow. Naive consciousness
sees causality as a static, established fact,
and thus is deceived in its perception.
(1974: 43-4)

Freire argues that oppressed and subjugated people
lack a critical understanding of their reality. To
them, the world is something which is fixed and to
which they must adapt. This view is supported by an
oppressive social structure which has a vested
interest in objectifying the world, making all
aspects of a person's situation appear 'natural' and
therefore unalterable. The first step towards
critical understanding is to appreciate the
distinction between the world of nature (which is
unalterable) and the world of culture (which is a
social construction and thereby alterable). Figure
9.1 below is a reproduction of a drawing which
Freire used with a literacy discussion group or
'culture circle'.
    The group co-ordinator initiates the debate by
distinguishing between culture and nature in the
situation which is depicted. For example, the
participants make a distinction between the feathers
of the bird as nature or culture. While the
feathers are on the bird they belong to the world of
nature, after the bird is killed and the feathers
are transformed into decorative headware, they
belong to the world of culture. The 'culture
circle', discusses a variety of pictorially
represented situations such as these, always with an
emphasis on how culture is created and transmitted
and on the possibility of democratising culture.

Figure 9.1: An illustration used by Freire

Source: Freire, 1974:66

Literacy makes sense only in these terms, as the
consequence of men's beginning to reflect about
their own capacity for reflection, about the
world, about their position in the world, about
their work, about their power to transform the
world, about the encounter of consciousness –
about literacy itself, which thereby ceases to
be something external and becomes a part of
them, comes as a creation from within them.   I
can see validity only in a literacy program in
which men understand words in their true
significance : as a force to transform the
world.   As illiterate men discover the
relativity of ignorance and of wisdom, they
destroy one of the myths by which false elites
have manipulated them.   (1974:81)

Appreciating the distinction between nature and
culture in the context of learning to read and write
constitutes a basis for problematising previously

taken-for-granted aspects of everyday life.
Problems such as housing, clothing, diet, health,
education and so on, are now seen as problems which
can be transformed by democratisation.

Horton and Freire have many things in common,
they both believe in the liberating potential of
education, especially when the critical analysis of
experience is linked with action upon the world to
transform it. They both work with disadvantaged and
oppressed groups and their methods are overtly
politicising. Naturally, their political activities
sparked a reaction from those with an interest in
maintaining the status quo - Freire was sent into
exile and Highlander was repeatedly attacked by the
Ku Klux Klan and eventually its charter was revoked
by the State of Tennessee (it continued to operate
under a new charter).

Adult educators frequently question the
relevance of Freire to the circumstances of
non-disadvantaged groups. However, Freire certainly
considered dominant groups to be oppressed, at least
in the psychological sense of having inauthentic
personal identities - inauthentic in that they have
become agents of oppression. This gives them a dual
status as both dominators and dominated. Freire
writes about the well-intentioned professionals who
discover the violence of their acts of invasion:
'Those who make this discovery face a difficult
alternative: they feel the need to renounce
invasion, but patterns of domination are so
entrenched within them that this renunciation would
become a threat to their own identities'
(1972:125). This can be illustrated by considering
the response of men to women's demands for equality
in the workplace. Many male professionals have
recently taken an interest in understanding the
'world view' of women. Now this can be done in the
interests of domination, in which case the male
professionals would learn 'about' women, or in the
interests of liberation, where the male
professionals would develop a critical awareness of
the dynamics of gender identity. There are many
instances like this in adult education and training,
that is, where there is a clear choice between
critical understanding, where the 'knower' is
implicated in the situation, and a purely technical
understanding, where the 'knower' remains detached
from the situation and maintains the posture of an
onlooker.

Indeed, this is a central issue in adult
education and it has a direct bearing on how we

conceive the ideal adult learner. Both Brookfield
and Mezirow, for example, have re-formulated earlier
conceptualisations of the self-directed learner to
include the idea of critical awareness.

Mezirow has his own version of
'conscientisation', he refers to a similar process
labelled 'perspective transformaton' which is:

> ...the emancipatory process of becoming
> critically aware of how and why the structure of
> psycho-cultural assumptions has come to
> constrain the way we see ourselves and our
> relationships, reconstituting this structure to
> permit a more inclusive and discriminating
> integration of experience and acting upon these
> new understandings. It is the learning process
> by which adults come to recognize their
> culturally induced dependency roles and
> relationships and the reasons for them and take
> action to overcome them. (1983:125)

Later he links this process with a re-formulation of
the concept of andragogy (Table 9.1).

It is worth comparing his 'Charter for
andragogy' with Knowles' distinction between
andragogy and pedagogy. Mezirow's 'Charter'
specifies a set of precepts for adult educators
which are targeted at fostering self-direction.
However, this is self direction with a new
complexion - it includes the idea of critical
awareness. A mature, self-directed learner is able
to make a commitment to learning on the basis of a
knowledge of genuine alternatives. Critically aware
learners are in touch with their authentic needs - a
characteristic which, incidentally, makes the adult
educator's task so much easier because the
problematic of meeting needs (as discussed earlier)
evaporates.

Brookfield follows a similar line in exploring
the concept of self-directedness.

> As the mode of learning characteristic of adults
> who are in the process of realizing their
> adulthood, self-directed learning is concerned
> much more with the internal change of
> consciousness than with the external management
> of instructional events. This consciousness
> involves an appreciation of the contextuality of
> knowledge and an awareness of the culturally
> constructed form of value frameworks, belief

Table 9.1: A charter for andragogy (Mezirow)

---

1) progressively decrease the learner's dependency on the educator;
2) help the learner to understand how to use learning resources - especially the experience of others, including the educator, and how to engage others in reciprocal learning relationships;
3) assist the learner to define his/her learning needs - both in terms of immediate awareness and of understanding the cultural and psychological assumptions influencing his/her perceptions of needs;
4) assist learners to assume increasing responsibility for defining their learning objectives, planning their own learning program and evaluating their progress;
5) organize what is to be learned in relationship to his/her current personal problems, concerns and levels of understanding;
6) foster learner decision making/select learner-relevant learning experiences which require choosing, expand the learner's range of options, facilitate taking the perspectives of others who have alternative ways of understanding;
7) encourage the use of criteria for judging which are increasingly inclusive and differentiating in awareness, self-reflexive and integrative of experience;
8) foster a self-corrective reflexive approach to learning - to typifying and labelling, to perspective taking and choosing, and to habits of learning and learning relationships;
9) facilitate problem posing and problem solving, including problems associated with the implementation of individual and collective action; recognition of relationships between personal problems and public issues;
10) reinforce the self-concept of the learner as a learner and doer by providing for progressive mastery; a supportive climate with feedback to encourage provisional efforts to change and to take risks; avoidance of competitive judgement of performance; appropriate use of mutual support groups;
11) emphasize experiential, participative and projective instructional methods; appropriate use of modelling and learning contracts;

Table 9.1 (cont'd)
A charter for andragogy (Mezirow)

---

12) make the moral distinction between helping the
learner understand his/her full range of choices
and how to improve the quality of choosing vs
encouraging the learner to make a specific
choice.

Source: Mezirow, 1983:136-7

> systems, and moral codes that influence
> behaviour and the creation of social
> structures... This most fully adult form of
> self-directed learning is one in which critical
> reflection on the contextual and contingent
> aspects of reality, the exploration of
> alternative perspectives and meaning systems,
> and the alteration of personal and social
> circumstances are all present. (1985a:15)

Both Brookfield and Mezirow have introduced a social
dimension to the concept of self-directed learning.
They admit that there are contraints on learning
which originate in the social structure and which
become internalised by the learner. This is their
point of contact with the more radical adult
educators such as Lovett et al (1983) Freire (1972)
Gelpi (1979) and Griffin (1983) and it separates
them quite sharply from the humanistic point of
view. By way of summary, Table 9.2 contrasts the
critical awareness and humanistic traditions in
terms of their stance on a number of key adult
education issues; the nature of self-directed
learning, needs-based provision, equity and access,
and the relationship between teachers and learners.
There is something incomplete about Brookfield
and Mezirow's analysis of critical awareness. The
reason, I think, is that they have depoliticised the
idea. They focus inwardly, as it were, on the
liberation of the learner and they very much stand
on the fence when it comes to organising collective
action. 'Our function is not to lead or organize
for collective action but to help learners become
aware of the cultural contradictions that oppress
them...' (Mezirow, 1985: 29). However, Freire
argues that an unmasking of reality needs to be
followed by critical intervention in order to
transform it. For him, thought and action are
indissoluble aspects of a single dialectical process
(praxis). Mere reflection is nothing but

Table 9.2: Contrasting traditions in the framing of issues in adult education

	Self-directed learning	Needs-based provision	Equity and Access	Teacher/learner relationship
The humanistic tradition	This occurs when learners determine goals and objectives, locate appropriate resources, plan their learning strategies and evaluate the outcomes. It is the appropriate way for mature adults to learn. It ensures freedom, autonomy, independence, student centredness and relevance. Learning is the responsibility of the learner - no one can learn for someone else.	Adult educators have a responsibility to meet the expressed needs of learners. These can be identified in a variety of ways: through responses to course offerings, group discussions, questionnaires, local government statistics, student planning committees, etc. It is the responsibility of individuals and groups of individuals to express their needs.	Adult education is characterised by open access to courses. Management structures and administrative practices ensure that access is guaranteed for those who seek it. It is the responsibility of the individual to exercise his/her right to learn as an adult.	The teacher is a "facilitator" of learning. This means having empathy with and trust in the learner, being genuine with the learner, and being open, caring and non-judgemental. This enables the learner to express his/her needs and it ensures that the larger group overcomes its conflicts. Here, learning is premised on individual freedom.
The critical awareness tradition	Autonomy and freedom is not to be found in the mastery of techniques and procedures for self learning. Much of the literature documenting self-directed learning is questionable on the grounds of its middle-class bias, both because of the populations surveyed and the nature of the survey and interview techniques. Self-direction should include the element of critical awareness of the social and cultural constraints impinging on one's behaviour.	The expressed needs of learners may have nothing at all to do with the objective educational needs of a group or community. Learners and potential learners are not always in a position to articulate their needs and thus may be unaware of the range of possibilities from which to choose. The needs-meeting paradigm is an aspect of the free market approach and it contains all the social and political trappings that go with it.	An educational provision which relies on self selection will widen, not narrow, educational and cultural gaps in society. Research on participation in adult education shows consistently that students are young, middle class and well educated. Adult education institutions need to actively recruit non-traditional students if the goal of equity is to be realised. They need to identify the social and cultural barriers to participation.	The teacher and learner enter a dialogue based on mutual trust. However the teacher plays an active role in challenging the learner's presuppositions - and confusion, uncertainty and ambiguity may result. Teaching and learning is a collaborative enterprise and the teacher does not have a monopoly on the right to challenge and intervene.

verbalism. It becomes an empty word, one which cannot denounce the world, for denunciation is impossible without a commitment to transform, and there is no transformation without action' (Freire, 1972:61). By way of contrast, pure action without reflection is nothing but activism - action for its own sake, which prevents dialogue and liberation.

Whether or not one subscribes to Freire's position, there is nevertheless a sense in which Brookfield and Mezirow fail to address the issue of action following from critical awareness. There is an implicit liberal tradition in their writing; that more perceptive and better educated (in their sense) individuals magically produce a more just and equitable society.

The relationship between critical awareness and action has been foregrounded elsewhere - in the domain of adult education research. Participatory or action research has been actively sponsored by adult education agencies such as the International Council for Adult Education (ICAE). The impetus for this has come partly from a sense of disquiet about research techniques which mimic the procedures of physical science (i.e. experimental control, hypothetico-deductive method) and partly from a political commitment to popular involvement in social research. The thrust of the ICAE's project is to link social and educational research to economic and social development, particularly in the Third World. One aspect of the project is to develop a view about how best to approach social and educational enquiry. Carr and Kemmis (1983), although working quite independently of the ICAE project, have sketched a scenario for research which has as its core the fusion of critical awareness and action. Their version of critical awareness has much in common with that of Brookfield and Mezirow, but they proceed a step further and explore the research implications of a commitment to the idea of being critically aware.

Carr and Kemmis (1983) and Mezirow (1983) adopt a common starting point in using Habermas' (1972) distinction between instrumental, practical and emancipatory knowledge. Instrumental knowledge allows us to control the environment. It is the type of knowledge which is commonly generated by empirical-analytic or natural sciences, where the researcher is an objective observer whose task is to identify cause-effect relationships. Practical knowledge helps us to understand the environment.

It does so by providing interpretations of actions and events which can inform and guide our practical judgement. Emancipatory knowledge helps us to break free from the taken-for-granted assumptions which guide our everyday behaviours and which distort our self-understanding. This type of knowledge is formed through a critique of the historical and social forces which shape our consciousness. It is this type of critique which Freire encouraged in his culture circles. It is also a characteristic of the critical social sciences. (e.g. Marx's theory of society and Freud's metapsychology) and it is advocated by Carr and Kemmis as the basis for emancipatory action research.

Carr and Kemmis set out to provide a rationale for the view that educational research should be construed as a form of critical social science where teachers are researchers in the sense that they systematically reflect on their practice. Their reflection, of course, must be 'critical':

.   It must provide ways of distinguishing ideas and interpretations which are systematically distorted by ideology from those which are not, and provide a view of how distorted self-understandings can be overcome.
.   It must be concerned to identify and expose those aspects of the existing social order which frustrate rational change, and must be able to offer theoretical accounts which enable teachers (and other participants) to become aware of how they may be overcome.   (1983:158)

The notion of 'critical' reflection is a key one for Carr and Kemmis and they proceed to demonstrate how the method they propose ensures a critical perspective. Their method, somewhat disappointingly, turns out to be remarkably simple – it consists of the notion of a spiral of self reflection:

.   to develop a plan of action to improve what is already happening,
.   to act to implement the plan,
.   to observe the effects of action in the context in which it occurs, and
.   to reflect on these effects as a basis for further planning, subsequent action and so on, through a succession of cycles. (Kemmis and McTaggart, 1982:7)

Critical awareness

The Action Research Planner, developed by Kemmis and
McTaggart (1982), details the sequence of steps in
the action research spiral - it is essentially a
checklist of what to do when carrying out action
research. It is certainly useful as a basis for
reflecting on practice, and it certainly encourages
a critical attitude towards practice - but there is
a notable gap between the promise of social and
political enlightenment and the rather mundane
advice to attend to questions like 'What is
happening now?' 'In what sense is this
problematic?' 'Who is affected?' 'With whom must I
negotiate?' 'Am I reflecting on the issues?' 'What
rethinking of the general idea or problem is called
for?'
    Carr and Kemmis advance an elegant and
sophisticated rationale for emancipatory action
research. Ultimately however, they are caught in
the same void as Habermas - between the idea of a
critical social or educational science and its
concrete realisation. The Action Research Planner
constitutes an attempt to give concrete expression
to the actions carried out by an action researcher -
but the steps and procedures to be followed are
general, designed to fit almost any teaching
situation. The point is that it is not possible to
know in advance whether the recommended steps will
or will not lead to a critique of a given situation
and a commitment to improve it. Action research as
a method is not (as Carr and Kemmis claim)
intrinsically critical.
    There is a general tendency among advocates of
the 'critical awareness' approach to emphasise the
importance of method and procedure at the expense of
content and direction (this does not apply to
Horton). For example Freire's distinction between
banking education and problem-posing education is
essentially a distinction between different methods
of learning, one necessarily oppressive, the other
necessarily liberating.

    Banking education (for obvious reasons)
    attempts, by mythicizing reality, to conceal
    certain facts which explain the way men exist in
    the world; problem-posing education sets itself
    the task of de-mythologizing. Banking education
    resists dialogue; problem-posing education
    regards dialogue as indispensable to the act of
    cognition which unveils reality. Banking
    education treats students as objects of
    assistance; problem-posing education makes them

150

critical thinkers. Banking education inhibits
creativity and domesticates (although it cannot
completely destroy) the intentionality of
conciousness by isolating consciousness from the
world, thereby denying men their ontological and
historical vocation of becoming more fully
human. Problem-posing education bases itself on
creativity and stimulates true reflection and
action upon reality, thereby responding to the
vocation of men as beings who are authentic only
when engaged in inquiry and creative
transformation. In sum: banking theory and
practice, as immobilizing and fixating forces,
fail to acknowledge men as historical beings;
problem-posing theory and practice take man's
historicity as their starting point. (1972:56)

Lovett (et al) denies the validity of this
distinction and claims that many features of
so-called banking education (for example, that the
teacher teaches and the students are taught) are not
intrinsically oppressive at all. Furthermore Lovett
defends the idea of vigorous, ordered and sustained
schooling '... education aiming to promote the
eradication of class division must include, at the
very least, some old-fashioned instruction, set into
an ordered curriculum, which includes basic
information and skills required to execute necessary
management tasks' (1983:145). Lovett challenges the
critical awareness approach on two counts. Firstly,
that questions of pedagogic method are secondary,
and that the overall purpose of the education is
what really matters (i.e. the content of learning
needs to fit the political aspirations of the
learners). Secondly, that oppression does not
simply evaporate through learners psychologically
re-orienting themselves to the world (i.e. unmasking
the myths upon which oppression is based). Lovett
makes this last point forcefully in his reaction to
the rhetoric of action research:

'Most of this is pure moralism: the liberation
of more and more people's efforts is not the
problem, since efforts are wasted without a
macro-economic strategy that can co-ordinate
them successfully, which is precisely what is
lacking; the notion of a 'right' to create
knowledge is absurd unless it is qualified by
some criteria distinguishing knowledge from
error and allowing the construction of
hierarchies of knowledge for the elaboration of

> theory; criteria, in other words, concerning the
> ability to create knowledge; and to hold that
> 'people can not be developed', is a rejection of
> the crucial determining role of education, at an
> individual level, and of macro-social change in
> human history – it is also, more importantly,
> false.   (1983:109)

Lovett's case is quite compelling, the more so
because of his well documented activities with
working class communities. His concern is with the
way in which adult learning, as a process which
leads to critical awareness, is portrayed as a
powerful force for social change. From the
standpoint of a psychology of adult learning
'critical awareness' is certainly a valuable
outcome. However it is a mistake to link this, as
an outcome, with any particular method of learning.
In particular, one should avoid the premature
dissolution of the distinction between teachers and
taught: 'Teachers must avoid the kind of autocracy
which undermines any democratic sensibility, but
they must, nevertheless, teach and include in their
teaching much of the best of what has been handed
down by centuries of intellectual contest and
co-operation.'   (1983:144)

Chapter Ten

CONCLUDING COMMENT: PSYCHOLOGY AS A FOUNDATION
DISCIPLINE IN ADULT EDUCATION

Psychology is frequently used as a foundation
discipline in the training of adult educators. This
is because it addresses those questions which
naturally emerge from an engagement with adult
teaching and learning. What motivates students to
attend classes? Through what processes do adults
learn best? How can I adjust my teaching practices
to take into account the learning styles of my
students? How can I encourage the formation of a
cohesive and supportive group? Can I make sense of
the expressed anxieties and concerns of my
students? What can I do to help those students who
experience difficulties in learning? Much of the
psychological literature has some bearing on each of
these questions, and others like them. However, it
is not at all clear how the practitioner should
proceed to apply the output of this literature to
the everyday activity of teaching adults. In this
respect there appear to be at least three available
options, each of them corresponding to a different
motive within the practitioner; to control events in
the learning environment, to interpret and influence
events, or to gain a critical understanding of
events and one's actions in relation to them.

Control

The desire for control among adult educators (which
is natural enough and quite understandable), is
often linked with a particular view about the
relationship between theory and practice. As a
foundation discipline, psychology is viewed as
providing a base of rules and principles which can
be unequivocally applied to practice. The
practitioner who holds such a view, however, is
likely to be disappointed with what psychology can

offer. The reasons for this have to do with the way
in which 'scientific psychology' generates
knowledge. As a science, psychology is very much
concerned with prediction and control, and to this
end seeks to identify cause-effect relationships.
However there are a number of factors which limit
the direct practical application of such knowledge.
Firstly, psychological experiments which adopt the
methods of natural science are characterised by what
Egan (1984) calls 'phenomena insensitivity'. That
is, while the methods are scientific, it may be at
the cost of distorting and/or narrowing the
phenomenon being investigated - so much that the
results have little direct applicability outside the
experimental context or the theoretical concerns of
the experiment. This is an argument advanced by
Usher (1986) and it is neatly expressed in Harre's
critique of social psychology:

> Psychologists have frequently supposed that one
> can divide up socially meaningful phenomena into
> basic non-meaningful units between which they
> have sought the kinds of correlations which
> Boyle and Hooke found between the pressures and
> volumes of gases. Let me give you an example.
> There have been studies of the development of
> liking between human beings. Psychologists have
> sought to investigate this process by
> identifying elementary features of the
> liking-generating process and studying them
> independently of all other features of a real
> situation of liking. They have isolated the
> frequency with which a person is confronted with
> another person as an element in the formation of
> liking between people. And then they have
> attempted to study the effect of frequency of
> meeting on the development of liking in an
> apparently 'pure' case. To this end, people
> were asked to report on the way in which their
> liking of nonsense syllables had changed with
> the frequency of presentation of such syllables.
>
> It should be clear that the most elementary
> examination of the social interaction which
> produces feelings of liking or disliking between
> people involves intimately and inextricably
> other elements besides mere frequency.
> Frequency is equivocal in social meaning. The
> notion of frequency by itself is not a social
> concept. It is an element which lacks the level
> of meaning at which liking and similar concepts
> apply.   (1974:249)

Of course, not all psychological experiments are open to such a challenge. Nevertheless, the problem of 'operationally' defining concepts like 'panic', 'obedience', 'conformity', and 'aggression', so that they can be measured in an experiment, is a factor limiting the generalisability and practical application of many research findings.

A related feature of psychological experiments is that they are conducted under controlled conditions. The experimenter achieves control either directly (which is the case with Skinner's laboratory experiments) or indirectly through, say, sampling techniques which select or randomise those variables which potentially confound the results. For example, an educational psychologist may be interested in plotting the effectiveness of a particular teaching strategy for subjects with different learning styles. This could be accomplished by holding the teaching strategy constant across two groups composed of subjects who differed only in their learning styles (i.e. not differing on factors such as sex, age, intelligence, ethnic grouping). The aim would be to arrive at some statement such as 'Teaching strategy 'X' is more effective for field dependents, all other things being equal'. A commonly perceived problem with applying this knowledge is that in everyday life 'all other things' are rarely, if ever, 'equal'. And in everyday life the extent of control is somewhat less than in a psychological experiment. But this misses the point – the very strength of a psychological experiment is its capacity to isolate variables for systematic study – and this means controlling other variables.

The position of psychology in this respect is not unique. For example, the laws and principles of other foundation disciplines such as physics or biology are characteristically qualified by expressions like 'all other things being constant'. And yet very few would deny the importance and relevance of physics and biology to the practices of engineering and medicine respectively. However, it is a mistake to assume that the knowledge derived from controlled experiments will necessarily lead to greater control of the environment.

A large component of the practitioner's skill consists of the ability to anticipate, recognise and compensate for the range of variables operating in a given context. Given this, the value of 'scientific

psychology' becomes somewhat clearer. It is the
corpus of experimental findings in a given area
which identifies for the practitioner the range of
likely variables operating and the subtleties of
their interaction. This can be illustrated with
reference to the corpus of research findings on the
effectiveness of different teaching methods (see
Gage, 1976). If practitioners approach this
literature looking for a set of generalisations to
guide practice, they will invariably be frustrated.
Nevertheless the literature is valuable in that it
alerts practitioners to the range of variables
influencing the effectiveness of a teaching method.
In the first instance, whether or not a teaching
method is effective will depend largely upon how
'effectiveness' is measured. There are a bevy of
contenders here: motivation, recall, understanding,
ability to learn, creativity, attitude change, etc.
There are also different ways of measuring each of
these factors. For example, attitude change can be
measured using a questionnaire, interview, or some
kind of behavioural index, and it can be measured
immediately, in the short term, or over a longer
period of time. In addition to these measurement
variables there are a host of factors to consider
such as the subject matter being taught, student
ability, age, sex, ethnicity, the teacher's
personality, size of class - all of which have been
the focus of experimental enquiry. The value of
this research is that it supplies the practitioner
with a complex array of variables to consider when
evaluating the appropriateness of a given teaching
method in a given context. Used in this way
psychology helps us to interpret and influence
events in the learning environment, rather than
control them.

Interpretation and influence

Usher (1986) advocates the application of
therapy-derived theories to an understanding of
adult teaching and learning. Unlike 'scientific'
psychologies the approach of these theories is
hermeneutic, that is, they seek to interpret
behaviour and stimulate insight, awareness and
understanding. Freudian psychoanalysis and
humanistic clinical psychology (see Chapters 2 and
3) are examples of this type of theory. Usher
argues that the activities of therapists and
counsellors are more like the activities of teachers
than are the experimental manipulations of the

scientific psychologists. Both the therapist and
the educator are concerned with interpreting ongoing
actions and events and adjusting their actions
accordingly. Unlike the notions of 'prediction' and
'control', the terms 'interpretation' and
'influence' imply that the teacher (or therapist) is
engaged in a reflexive dialogue with the student (or
client). Thus the activity of teaching requires
practical judgement in a context where the variables
operating are unable to be measured or controlled.
This practical judgement, and the action which flows
from it, is informed by psychological theory in the
sense that the theory provides a framework for
interpreting events.

The difficulty with this model of the
relationship between psychology and adult teaching
and learning, is that there exist competing
theoretical frameworks which offer quite different
interpretations of similar events. For example, an
adult student may express disappointment with a
course, claiming that it has failed to meet his/her
need for a stimulating, exciting and challenging
experience. A psychoanalytic interpretation may
hold that such a demand is unrealistic, and is
really an expression of an infantile wish to be
totally loved and cared for unconditionally. A
humanistic interpretation may hold that the same
person is expressing a desire for growth and
fulfilment, which is a natural and healthy thing to
do. There are practitioners who remain undaunted by
such opposing interpretations claiming that they
operate by synthesising different theoretical
perspectives, but Reese and Overton, among others,
have reservations about the possibility of this
occurring:

> Theories built upon radically different models
> are logically independent and cannot be
> assimilated to each other. They reflect
> representations of different ways of looking at
> the world and as such are incompatible in their
> implications. Different world views involve
> different understanding of what is knowledge and
> hence of the meaning of truth. Therefore
> synthesis is at best confusing.   (1970:144)

One may remonstrate that practitioners are not bound
by the rigours of theory construction in Reese and
Overton's sense - and this is certainly true - but
they do reflect upon or 'theorise' about their
practice. That is, they form a relatively coherent

Concluding comment

'world view' which informs their practical
judgement. Such a 'world view' may be 'naive' or it
may be more or less based upon a knowledge of
psychology, philosophy or educational theory. A
critical understanding of psychology can assist the
practitioner to re-examine the 'world view' he or
she has adopted, to re-evaluate and re-formulate it.
This was referred to earlier as a third option in
linking psychology with adult teaching and learning.

Critical understanding

There are two senses in which adult education
practitioners can have a critical (psychological)
understanding of their practice. The first sense
has been outlined above - practitioners can
interpret (rather than accept at face value) actions
and events in the learning environment. In the
second sense, practitioners can analyse the
psychological 'world view' they adopt when
interpreting those actions and events. This is
where a critical understanding of competing
psychological theories is important, which means
analysing the conceptual weaknesses and
contradictions within each theory, evaluating
whether each theory is supported by the evidence,
assessing the success of the practices promoted by
each theory, and finally, being aware of the social,
historical and political origins and impact of each
theory. By scrutinising their psychological 'world
views' practitioners are better able to recognise
and appreciate the world views of others and they
are in a better position to articulate their goals
and purposes as adult educators. There are many
areas in adult education where a conflict of world
views, especially between the teacher and student,
is commonplace. I have in mind here areas such as
literacy, numeracy, second language learning, worker
education, 'second chance' education, education for
the unemployed, health education and so forth. In
all of these areas there is a high probability that
competing world views will emerge. Symptomatic of
this will be differences in opinion among the
students, or between the students and the teacher,
about what constitutes relevant content, appropriate
teaching methods, the role and responsibilities of
the teacher, and the purposes of the program.
    While it is true that a commitment to a
particular psychological 'world view' provides a
powerful interpretive framework for adult educators,

they need also to be aware of alternative 'world views'. A critical understanding of a range of psychological 'world views' is preferable to a blind faith in any single one. This does not mean that adult educators should adopt a chameleon-like character, shifting colours as the environmental circumstances dictate - it only means that they should be aware of their 'world view' and understand its limitations in the context of the alternatives available.

This text has adopted a critical posture towards selected psychological theories and research findings. The purpose has not been to dissuade adult educators from further psychological enquiry - but to encourage them to approach their enquiry with a critical spirit. Approached in this way, psychological theory and research is better able to foster among adult educators a capacity for making informed choices which are defensible on rational, practical and moral grounds.

BIBLIOGRAPHY

Adams, F. (1975). Unearthing seeds of fire.
Charlotte, North Car, Blair.

Allman, P. (1982). New perspectives on the adult,
an argument for lifelong education. _International
Journal of Lifelong Education_, 1 (1), 41-52.

Allport, G. (1961). _Pattern and growth in
personality_. New York: Holt, Rinehart and Winston.

Appel, M. and Golberg, L. (Eds.) (1977). _Topics in
cognitive development_. Vol. 1. Equilibration:
theory research and application. New York: Plenum
Press.

Appel, M. H., Presseisen, B. Z. & Goldstein, P.
(Eds.) (1978). _Topics in cognitive development_.
Vol. 2. Language and operational thought. New
York: Plenum Press.

Armistead, N. (Ed.) (1974). _Reconstructing social
psychology_. Middlesex: Penguin.

Armstrong, P. F. (1982). The needs meeting ideology
in liberal adult education. _The International
Journal of Lifelong Education_. 1 (4), 293-321.

Asch, S. (1956). Studies of independence and
conformity: a minority of one against a unanimous
majority. _Psychological monographs_, 9 (complete
volume).

Bales, R. (1950). _Interaction process analysis: A
method for the study of small groups_. Cambridge,
Mass: Addison-Wesley.

Bales, R. (1958). Task roles and social roles in problem solving groups. In E. Maccoby, M. Newcomb and E. Hartley (Eds.) Readings in social psychology. New York: Holt, Rinehart and Winston, 437-47.

Baltes, P. (1968). Longitudinal and cross-sectional sequences in the study of age and generation effects. Human Development, 11, 145-171.

Bandura, A. (1969). Principles of behaviour modification. New York: Holt, Rinehart and Winston.

Basseches, M. (1984). Dialectical thinking and adult development. New Jersey: Ablex Publishing.

Basseches, M. (1986). Comments on social cognition in adulthood: A dialectical perspective. Educational Gerontology, 12 (4), 327-34.

Bengtsson, J. (1979). The work/leisure/education life cycle. In T. Schuller and J. Megarry (Eds.), Recurrent education and lifelong learning. London: Kogan Page, 17-30.

Bennis, W. and Shephard, H. (1956). A theory of group development. Human Relations, 9, 415-437.

Berger, P. & Luckmann, T. (1967). The social construction of reality. Harmondsworth: Penguin.

Bion, W. (1968). Experiences in groups. London: Tavistock.

Bloom, B. (1956). Taxonomy of educational objectives. London: Longmann.

Boud, D. (1981). Developing student autonomy in learning. London: Kogan Page.

Boud, D. (1987). A facilitator's view of adult learning. In D. Boud and V. Griffin (Eds.) Appreciating adults learning: From the learner's perspective. London: Kogan Page, 222-239.

Boud, D., Keogh, R. & Walker, D. (Eds.) (1985). Reflection: Turning experience into learning. London: Kogan Page.

Bibliography

Boyer, D. (1984). Malcolm Knowles and Carl Rogers. A comparison of andragogy and student-centered education. Lifelong Learning. 7(4), 17-20.

Bradford, L. (Ed.) (1978). Group development. La Jolla: University Associates.

Bradford, L., Gibb, J. and Benne, K. (1964). T-group theory and laboratory method: Innovation in re-education. New York: Wiley.

Braginsky, B. & Braginsky, D. (1974). Mainstream psychology: A critique. New York: Holt, Rinehart and Winston.

Brookfield, S. (1981). The adult learning iceberg: a critical review of the work of Allen Tough. Adult Education, 54 (2), 110-18.

Brookfield, S. (1983). Adult learners, adult education and the community. Milton Keynes: Open University Press.

Brookfield, S. (1985a). Self-directed learning: a critical review of research. In S. Brookfield (Ed.) Self directed learning: From theory to practice. San Francisco: Jossey-Bass, 5-16.

Brookfield, S. (1985b). A critical definition of adult education. Adult Education Quarterly, 36 (1), 44-9.

Brookfield, S. (1985c). Self-directed learning: a conceptual and methodological exploration. Studies in the Education of Adults, 17 (1), 19-32.

Brookfield, S. (1986). Understanding and facilitating adult learning. San Francisco: Jossey-Bass.

Broughton, J. M. (1981). Piaget's structural developmental psychology: ideology-critique and the possibility of a critical developmental theory. Human Development, 24, 382-411.

Bruner, J. (1966). The process of education. Cambridge: Harvard University Press.

Bruner, J. (1971). The relevance of education. London: George Allen and Unwin.

Buck-Morss, S. (1975). Socio-economic bias in Piaget's theory and its implications for cross-cultural studies. Human Development, 18, 35-49.

Buehler, C. & Massarik, F. (Eds.) (1968). The course of human life. New York: Springer.

Buss, A. R. (1979). Dialectics, history and development: The historical roots of the individual - society dialectic. In P. Baltes and O. Brim (Eds.) Life-span development and behavior. Vol. 2. New York: Academic Press, 313-33.

Caffarella, R. & Caffarella, E. (1986). Self-directedness and learning contracts in adult education, Adult Education Quarterly, 36 (4), 226-234.

Callahan, E. & McCluskey, K. (Eds.) (1983). Lifespan developmental psychology: Non-normative life events. New York: Academic Press.

Carr, W. & Kemmis, S. (1983). Becoming critical: Knowing through action research. Waure Ponds: Deakin University Press.

Cartwright, D. & Zander, A. (1968). Group dynamics. New York: Harper & Row.

Cattell, R. (1963). Theory of fluid and crystallized intelligence: A critical experiment. Journal of Educational Psychology, 54 (1), 1-22.

Chickering, A. W. (1969). Education and identity. San Francisco: Jossey-Bass.

Chickering, A. W. (1978). The double bind of field dependence/independence in program alternatives for educational development. In S. Messick and Associates, Individuality in Learning. San Francisco: Jossey-Bass, 79-89.

Chickering, A. W. (Ed.) (1981). The modern American college. San Francisco: Jossey-Bass.

Chickering, A. W. (1983). Education and work - and human development. The Journal of Continuing Higher Education, 31 (2), 2-6.

Bibliography

Chickering, A. W. & Havighurst, R. (1981). The life cycle. In A. W. Chicerking (Ed.), op.cit., 16-50.

Chodorow, N. (1978). The reproduction of mothering: Psychoanalysis and the sociology of gender. Berkeley: University of California Press.

Chomsky, N. (1959). Review of 'Verbal Behavior' by B. F. Skinner. Language, 35 (1), 26-58.

Connell, R. W. (1983). Dr Freud and the course of history. In R W Connell, Which way is up? Essays on class, sex and culture. Sydney: George Allen and Unwin, 141-52.

Conti, G. (1985). The relationship between teaching style and adult student learning. Adult Education Quarterly, 35 (4), 220-28.

Conti, G. & Welborn, R. (1986). Teaching-learning styles and the adult learner. Lifelong Learning, 9 (8), 20-22.

Colarusso, C. & Nemiroff, A. (1981). Adult development. New York: Plenum Press.

Cooper, C. (Ed.) (1975). Theories of group processes. London: Wiley.

Cross, K. P. (1981). Adults as learners. San Francisco: Jossey-Bass.

Darkenwald, G. & Merriam, S. (1982). Adult education: Foundations of practice. New York: Harper and Row.

Datan, N. & Ginsberg, L. (Eds.) (1975). Lifespan developmental psychology: Normative life crises. New York: Academic Press.

Davis, R., Alexander, L. & Yelon, S. (1974). Learning system design. New York: McGraw-Hill.

Dean, G. & Dowling, W. (1987). Community development: An adult education model. Adult Education Quarterly, 37 (2), 78-9.

Delbecq, A., Van der Ven, A. & Gustafson, D. (1975). Group processes for program planning: A guide to nominal group and Delphi processes. Glenview, Illinois: Scott Foreman and Co.

164

Dixon, N. (1985). The implementation of learning style information. Lifelong Learning, 9 (3), 16-27.

Doise, W. (1978). Groups and individuals: Explanations in social psychology. Cambridge: Cambridge University Press.

Doise, W., Mugny, G. and Perret-Clermont, A. (1976). Social interaction and cognitive development: Further evidence. European Journal of Social Psychology, 6 (2), 245-47.

Douglas, T. (1983). Groups. London: Tavis.

Dunphy, D. (1968). Phases, roles and myths in self-analytic groups. Journal of Applied Behavioral Science, 4, 195-226.

Egan, K. (1984). Education and psychology. London: Methuen.

Elkind, D. & Flavell, J. (Eds.) (1969). Studies in cognitive development. Essays in honor of Jean Piaget. New York: Oxford University Press.

Entwistle, N. (1981). Styles of learning and teaching. New York: Wiley.

Erikson, E. H. (1959). Identity and the life cycle. Psychological Issues, 1 (1) (Monograph No. 1).

Erikson, E. H. (1963). Childhood and society. New York: Norton.

Erikson, E. H. (Ed.) (1978). Adulthood. New York: Norton.

Feather, N. (1964). Acceptance and rejection of arguments in relation to attitude strength, critical ability and tolerance of inconsistency. Journal of Abnormal and Social Psychology, 69 (2), 127-36.

Flavell, J. (1963). The developmental psychology of Jean Piaget. New York: Van Nostrand.

Flavell, J. (1971). Stage-related properties of cognitive development. Cognitive Psychology, 2, 421-53.

Bibliography

Flavell, J. (1972). An analysis of cognitive developmental sequences. Genetic Psychology Monographs, 86, 279-350.

Flavell, J. & Wohlwill, J. (1969). Formal and functional aspects of cognitive development. In D Elkind and J Flavell (Eds.), op. cit 67-119.

Floyd, A. (1976). Cognitive styles. Milton Keynes: Open University Press.

Freire, P. (1972). Pedagogy of the oppressed. Harmondsworth: Penguin.

Freire, P. (1974). Education: The practice of freedom. London: Writers and Readers.

Freire, P. (1985). The politics of education: Culture, power and liberation. London: Macmillan.

Freud, S. (1949). An outline of psychoanalysis. New York: Norton.

Freud, S. (1953). Fragment of an analysis of a case of hysteria. In J. Strachey (Ed.). The standard edition of the complete psychological works of Sigmund Freud, Volume 7. London: Hogarth Press, 7-122.

Freud, S. (1958). A note on the unconscious in psychoanalysis. In J. Strachey, (Ed.). The standard edition of the complete psychological works of Sigmund Freud. Volume 12. London: Hogarth, 260-66.

Freud, S. (1963). Civilization and its discontents. London: Hogarth.

Freud, S. (1973a). Introductory lectures on psychoanalysis. Harmondsworth: Penguin.

Freud, S. (1973). New introductory lectures on psychoanalysis. Harmondsworth: Penguin.

Fromm, E. (1973). The crisis of psychoanalysis. Harmondsworth: Penguin.

Furst, E. (1981). Bloom's taxonomy of educational objectives for the cognitive domain: philosophy and educational issues. Review of Educational Research, 51 (4), 441-53.

Gage, N. L. (1976). The psychology of teaching methods. Chicago: NSSE.

Gelpi, E. (1979). A future for lifelong education. Vols. 1 and 2. Manchester: Manchester Monographs.

Gilligan, C. (1979). In a different voice. Cambridge: Harvard University Press.

Gilligan, C. & Kohlberg, L. (1978). From adolescence to adulthood: the re-discovery of reality in a post-conventional world. In M H Appel, et al (Eds.) op cit 125-36.

Goldstein, K. (1939). The organism. Boston: Beacon Press.

Goslin, D. A. (Ed.) (1969). Handbook of socialization theory and research. New York: Rand McNally.

Gould, R. (1972). The phases of adult life. The American Journal of Psychiatry, 129 (5), 521-31.

Gould, R. (1978). Transformations: Growth and change in adult life. New York: Simon and Schuster.

Goulet, L. R. & Baltes, P. B. (Eds.) (1970). Lifespan developmental psychology. New York: Academic Press.

Griffin, C. (1983). Curriculum theory in adult and lifelong education. London: Croom Helm.

Gronlund, N. E. (1978). Stating behavioral objectives for classroom instruction. New York: Macmillan.

Guglielmino, L. M. & Guglielmino, P. T. (1982). Self-directed learning readiness scale. Boca Raton, Guglielmino and Associates.

Habermas, J. (1972). Knowledge and human interests. London: Heinemann.

Habermas, J. (1979). Communication and the evolution of society. Boston: Beacon.

Hare, P. (1976). Handbook of small group research. London: The Free Press.

Bibliography

Harre, R. (1974). Blueprint for a new science. In
N Armistead (Ed.), Reconstructing social
psychology. Harmondsworth: Penguin, 240-58.

Hart, M. (1985). Thematization of power, the search
for common interests and self reflection: Towards a
comprehensive theory of emancipatory education.
International Journal of Lifelong Education, 4 (2),
119-34.

Hartree, A. (1984). Malcolm Knowles' theory of
andragogy: A critique. International Journal of
Lifelong Education, 3 (3), 203-10.

Havighurst, R. J. (1972). Developmental tasks and
education. (3rd ed.). New York: McKay.

Henry, R. M. (1980). A theoretical and empirical
analysis of reasoning in the socialisation of young
children. Human Development, 23, 105-25.

Heron, J. (1975). Six category intervention
analysis. Human Potential Research Project.
Surrey: University of Surrey.

Horn, J. and Cattell, R. (1967). Age differences in
fluid and crystallized intelligence. Acta
Psychologica, 26, 107-29.

Horn, J. and Cattell, R. (1968). Refinement and
test of the theory of fluid and crystallized
intelligence. Journal of Educational Psychology,
57, 253-70.

Horton, M. (1986). Seminar held at the Aboriginal
Training and Cultural Institute. Sydney, Australia.

Houle, C. (1972). The design of education. San
Francisco: Jossey-Bass.

Huberman, A. M. (1974). Some models of adult
learning and adult change. Strasbourg: Council of
Europe.

Jacoby, R. (1975). Social amnesia. Boston: Beacon.

Jahoda, M. (1977). Freud and the dilemmas of
psychology. London: Hogarth.

Jaques, D. (1984). Learning in groups. London:
Croom Helm.

Jarvis, P. (1983). Adult and continuing education: Theory and practice. London: Croom Helm.

Jarvis, P. (1984). Andragogy: A sign of the times, Studies in the Education of Adults, 16, 32-8.

Jarvis, P. (1987a). Meaningful and meaningless experience: towards an analysis of learning from life. Adult Education Quarterly, 57 (3), 164-72.

Jarvis, P. (1987b). Adult learning in the social context. London: Croom Helm.

Kasworm, C. (1983). Self-directed learning and lifespan development. International Journal of Lifelong Education, 2 (1), 29-46.

Kemmis, S. (1985). Action research and the politics of reflection. In D. Boud, et al. (Eds.) op.cit. 139-63.

Kemmis, S. & McTaggart, R. (1982). The action research planner. Waure Ponds: Deakin University Press.

Kimmel, D. C. (1980). Adulthood and ageing. New York: John Wiley.

Knowles, M. (1972). The modern practice of adult education. Chicago: Association Press.

Knowles, M. (1975). Self-directed learning. New York: Association Press.

Knowles, M. (1978). The adult learner: A neglected species. Houston: Gulf Publishing.

Knowles, M. (Ed.) (1984). Andragogy in action. San Francisco: Jossey-Bass.

Knox, A. (1977). Adult development and learning. San Francisco: Jossey-Bass.

Knox, A. (1979). Research insights into adult learning. In T. Schuller and J. Megarry (Eds.): Recurrent education and lifelong learning. London: Kogan, 57-79.

Kohlberg, L. (1969). Stage and sequence: The cognitive-development approach to socialisation. In D. Goslin (Ed.), op.cit, 347-480.

Bibliography

Kohlberg, L. (1971). From is to ought: How to commit the naturalistic fallacy and get away with it. In T. Mischel (Ed.), Cognitive development and epistemology. New York: Academic Press, 151-235.

Kohlberg, L. (1973-75). Moral judgement interview. Unpublished manuscript, Harvard Graduate School of Education.

Kohlberg, L. and Gilligan, C. (1971). The adolescent as a philospher: the discovery of the self in a post-conventional world. Daedalus, 100, 1051-86.

Kolb, D. (1976). The learning style inventory: Technical manual. Boston: McBer and Co.

Kolb, D. (1981). Learning styles and disciplinary differences. In A. W. Chickering (Ed.) op.cit, 232-55.

Kolb, D. (1984). Experiential learning. Englewood Cliffs, N.J.: Prentice-Hall.

Kolb, D. & Fry, R. (1975). Towards an applied theory of experiential learning. In C. Cooper (Ed.) op.cit, 33-57.

Kolb, D., Rubin, I. & McIntyre, J. (1984). Organizational psychology. New Jersey: Prentice-Hall.

Kramer, D. (1986). A life-span view of social cognition. Educational Gerontology, 12 (4), 277-90.

Labouvie-Vief, G. (1977). Adult cognitive development: In search of alternative interpretations. Merrill-Palmer Quarterly, 24 (4), 227-63.

Labouvie-Vief, G. (1980). Beyond formal operations: Uses and limits of pure logic in lifespan development. Human Development, 23, 141-61.

Lawson, K. (1975). Philosophical concepts and values in adult education. Nottingham: University of Nottingham.

Levinson, D. (1978). The seasons of a man's life. New York: Knopf.

Lewin, K. (1958). Group decision and social change. In E. Maccoby, M. Newcomb and E. Hartley (Eds.). Readings in Social Psychology. New York: Holt, Rinehart and Winston, 197-211.

Loevinger, J. (1976). Ego development. San Francisco: Jossey-Bass.

Long, H. (1983). Adult learning: Research and practice. New York: Cambridge.

Lovell, B. (1980). Adult learning. London: Croom Helm.

Lovett, T. (1975). Adult education, community development and the working class. London: Ward Lock.

Lovett, T., Clark, C. & Kilmurray, A. (1983). Adult education and community action. London: Croom Helm.

Lowenthal, M., Thurnher, M. & Chiriboga, D. (1977). Four stages of life. San Francisco: Jossey-Bass.

Lukes, S. (1973). Individualism. Oxford: Basil Blackwell.

McCoy, V. (1977). Adult life cycle change: How does growth affect our education needs? Lifelong Learning: The Adult Years, 31, 14-18.

MacDonald-Ross, M. (1975). 'Behavioural objectives: a critical review' in L. Dobson, T. Gear and A. Westoby (Eds.), Management in education. Vol. 2, Some techniques and systems. London: Ward Lock.

McGurk, H. (Ed.) (1978). Issues in childhood social development. London: Methuen.

McLeish, J., Matheson, W. & Park, J. (1973). The psychology of the learning group. London: Hutchinson & Co.

Malcolm, A. (1975). The tyranny of the group. New Jersey: Adams & Co.

Mann, R. (1967). Interpersonal styles and group development. New York: Wiley.

Marcuse, H. (1969). Eros and civilisation. London: Sphere Books.

Bibliography

Martin, J. (1980). Perspectives on person and society. Unpublished manuscript. Sydney: Macquarie University.

Maslow, A. (1968a). Towards a psychology of being. New York: Van Nostrand.

Maslow, A. (1968b). Some educational implications of the humanistic psychologies. Harvard Educational Review, 36, 685-96.

Mead, G. H. (1972). On social psychology. Selected papers edited by A. Strauss. Chicago: University of Chicago Press.

Melton, R. (1978). Resolution of conflicting claims concerning the effect of behavioural objectives on student learning. Review of Educational Research, 48 (2), 291-302.

Messick, S. & Associates. (1978). Individuality in learning. San Francisco: Jossey-Bass.

Mezirow, J. (1983). A critical theory of adult learning and education. In M. Tight (Ed.) Adult learning and education. London: Croom Helm, 124-38.

Mezirow, J. (1985). A critical theory of self-directed learning. In S. Brookfield (Ed.) op.cit., 17-30.

Milgram, S. (1965). Some conditions of obedience and disobedience to authority. Human Relations, 18 (1), 57-76.

Mills, T. (1964). Group transformation: An analysis of a learning group. Englewood Cliffs, N.J.: Prentice-Hall.

Mischel, T. (Ed.) (1971). Cognitive development and epistemology. New York: Academic Press.

Modgil, S. & Modgil, C. (1976). Piagetian research: Compilation and commentary (Vol. 6). Windsor: NFER Publishing.

Modgil, S. & Modgil, C. (1986). Lawrence Kohlberg: Consensus and controversy. London: Falmer Press.

Morelli, E. (1978). The sixth stage of moral development. Journal of Education, 7, 97-108.

Moreno, J. (1941). Foundations of sociometry, an introduction. Sociometry, 4, 15-35.

Moreno, J. (1953). Who shall survive? New York: Beacon.

Mugny, G. & Doise, W. (1978). Socio-cognitive conflict and structure of individual and collective performances. European Journal of Social Psychology, 8, 181-92.

Musgrove, F. (1977). Margins of the mind. London: Methuen.

Neugarten, B. L. (Ed.) (1968). Middle age and aging. Chicago: University of Chicago Press.

Newman, M. (1979). The poor cousin. London: George Allen and Unwin.

Nottingham Andragogy Group (1983). Towards a developmental theory of andragogy. Nottingham: University of Nottingham.

OECD (1973). Recurrent education: A strategy for lifelong learning. Paris.

OECD (1979). Recurrent education for the 1980s: Trends and policies. Paris: CERI.

Olmsted, M. & Hare, P. (1978). The small group. New York: Random House.

Pavlov, I. P. (1927). Conditioned reflexes. Trans. by G. V. Anrep. Oxford: Oxford University Press.

Perry, W. (1981). Cognitive and ethical growth: The making of meaning. In Chickering, A. (Ed.), op. cit. 76-116.

Peters, R. S. (1971). Moral development: A plea for pluralism. In. T. Mischel (Ed.), op. cit. 237-67

Piaget, J. (1954). The construction of reality in the child. New York: Basic Books.

Piaget, J. (1973). The child's conception of the world. London: Paladin.

Piaget, J. (1977a). The moral judgement of the child. Harmondsworth: Penguin.

Bibliography

Piaget, J. (1977b). Problems of equilibration. In M. H. Appel and L. S. Goldberg, (Eds.), op. cit. 3-13.

Piaget, J. (1978). The development of thought: Equilibration of cognitive structures. Oxford: Basil Blackwell.

Piaget, J. & Inhelder, B. (1956). The child's conception of space. London: Routledge and Kegan Paul.

Podeschi, R. & Pearson, E. (1986). Knowles and Maslow: Differences about freedom. Lifelong Learning, 9 (7), 16-18.

Reese, H. & Overton, W. (1970). Models of development and theories of development. In L. R. Goulet & P. B. Baltes (Eds.), op. cit. 116-45.

Reich, W. (1972). The sexual revolution. Vision Press.

Riegel, K.F. (1973). Dialectical operations: The final period of cognitive development. Human Development, 16, 346-70.

Riegel, K. F. (1976). The dialectics of human development. American Psychologist, Oct., 689-99.

Riegel, K. F. (1978). Psychology mon amour: A countertext. Boston: Houghton Mifflin.

Riegel, K. F. & Rosenwald, G. (Ed.) (1975). Structure and transformation. New York: Wiley.

Roazen, P. (1976). Erik H. Erikson. New York: Free Press.

Robinson, J. & Taylor, D. (1983). Behavioural objectives in training for adult education. International Journal of Lifelong Education, 2 (4), 355-70.

Rogers, C. (1951). Client-centred therapy. Boston: Houghton Mifflin.

Rogers, C. (1983). Freedom to learn for the 1980s. Columbus: Merrill.

Rotman, B. (1977). Jean Piaget: Psychologist of the real. Sussex: Harvester Press.

Salzberger-Wittenberg, I., Henry, G. & Osborne, E. (1983). The emotional experience of learning and teaching. London: Routledge and Kegan Paul.

Scannell, E. & Newstrom, J. (1983). More games trainers play. New York: McGraw Hill.

Schaie, K. (1965). A general model for the study of developmental problems. Psychological Bulletin, 64, 92-107.

Schaie, K. (1973). Methodological problems in descriptive developmental research on adulthood and aging. In J. Nesselroade and H. Reese (Eds.). Lifespan developmental psychology: Methodological issues. New York: Academic Press, 253-80.

Schaie, K. (1979). The primary mental abilities in adulthood: An exploration in the development of psychometric intelligence. In P. Baltes and O. Brim (Eds.). Lifespan development and behavior, Volume 2. New York: Academic Press, 68-115.

Schaie, K. (1983). Longitudinal studies of adult psychological development. New York: Guilford Press.

Schön, D. (1987). Educating the reflective practitioner. San Francisco: Jossey-Bass.

Schutz, W.C. (1955). What makes groups productive? Human Relations, 8, 429-65.

Shaw, M. (1981). Group dynamics. New York: McGraw Hill.

Sherif, M. (1935). The psychology of social norms. New York: Harper.

Shor, I. (1980). Critical teaching in everyday life. Boston: South End Press.

Simpson, E. L. (1974). Moral development research: A case study of scientific-cultural bias. Human Development, 17, 81-106.

Skinner, B.F. (1938). The behaviour of organisms: An experimental analysis. New York: Appleton-Century-Crofts.

Bibliography

Skinner, B. F. (1959). Science and human behaviour. New York: Macmillan.

Skinner, B. F. (1973). Beyond freedom and dignity. Harmondsworth: Penguin.

Smith, R. M. (1984). Learning how to learn. Milton Keynes: Open University Press.

Squires, G. (1981). Cognitive styles and adult learning. Nottingham: University of Nottingham.

Stevens-Long, J. (1979). Adult life: Developmental processes. Mayfield: Palo Alto.

Sullivan, E. V. (1977). A study of Kohlberg's structural theory of moral development: A critique of liberal social science ideology. Human Development, 20, 352-76.

Tennant, M. (1985a). 'Training adult educators: A case study', Forum of Education, 44 (2), 10-20.

Tennant, M. (1985b). The concept of 'need' in adult education. Australian Journal of Adult Education, 25 (2), 8-12.

Tennant, M. (1986). An evaluation of Knowles' theory of adult learning. International Journal of Lifelong Education, 5 (2), 113-22.

Thelen, H. and Dickerman, W. (1949). Stereotypes and the growth of groups. Educational Leadership, 6, 309-99.

Thompson, J. (1983). Learning liberation: Women's response to men's education. London: Croom Helm.

Thompson, J. (1985). Untitled paper presented at a AAAE Adult Education Seminar, March. Sydney.

Thompson, J. (Ed.) (1980). Adult education for a change. London: Hutchinson.

Tight, M. (Ed.) (1983). Adult learning and education. London: Croom Helm.

Tough, A. (1967). Learning without a teacher: A study of tasks and assistance during adult self-teaching projects. Toronto: Ontario Institute of Studies in Education.

Tough, A. (1968). Why adults learn: A study of the major reasons for beginning and continuing a learning project. Toronto: Ontario Institute for Studies in Education.

Tough, A. (1979). The adult's learning projects: A fresh approach to theory and practice in adult learning. Toronto: Ontario Institute for Studies in Education.

Tough, A. (1982). Intentional changes. Chicago: Follett.

Tough, A. (1983). Self-planned learning and major personal change. In M. Tight (Ed.), op. cit. 141-52.

Tucker, B. & Huerta, C. (1987). A study of developmental tasks as perceived by young adult Mexican-American females. Lifelong Learning, 10 (4), 4-7.

Tuckman, B. (1965). Developmental sequence in small groups. Psychological Bulletin, 63, 384-99.

UNESCO (1972). Learning to be: The world of education today and tomorrow (Faure Report). Paris.

UNESCO (1976). Foundations of lifelong education. Oxford: Pergamon Press.

Usher, R. (1986). The theory-practice problem and psychology as a foundation discipline in adult education. Proceedings of the Sixteenth Annual Conference of SCUTREA, University of Hull, 103-12.

Vaillant, G. (1977). Adaptation to life. Boston: Little Brown.

Wapner, S. (1978). Process and context in the conception of cognitive style. In S. Messick and Associates, op.cit., 79-89.

Watson, J. B. (1913). Psychology as the behaviorist views it. Psychological Review, 20, 158.

Weathersby, R. (1981). Ego development. In A. W. Chickering (Ed.), op. cit., 51-75.

Wiltshire, H. (1973). The concepts of learning and need in adult education. Studies in Adult Education, 5 (1), 26-30.

Bibliography

Witkin, H. (1950). Perception of the upright when the direction of the force acting on the body is changed. Journal of Experimental Psychology, 40, 93-106.

Witkin, H. (1978). Cognitive style in academic performance and in teacher-student relations. In S. Messick and Associates, op.cit., 38-72.

Witkin, H., Goodenough, D. and Karp, S. (1967). Stability of cognitive style from childhood to young adulthood. Journal of Personality and Social Psychology, 7, 291-300.

Witkin, H., Moore, C., Goodenough, D. & Cox, P. (1977). Field-dependent and field independent cognitive styles and their educational implications. Review of Educational Research, 47, (1), 1-64.

Wozniak, R. H. (1975). Dialecticism and structuralism: The philosophical foundation of Soviet psychology and Piagetian cognitive developmental theory. In K. Riegel and G. Rosenwald (Eds.), op. cit., 25-46.

Wrong, D. (1961). The oversocialised conception of man in modern sociology. American Sociological Review, 26 (2), 183-93.

Youniss, T. (1978). The nature of social development: A conceptual discussion of cognition. In H. McGurk (Ed.), op. cit., 203-27.

Zander, A. (1983). Making groups effective. San Francisco: Jossey-Bass.

Zeichner, K. and Liston, D. (1987). Teaching student teachers to reflect. Harvard Educational Review, 57 (1), 23-48.

INDEX

Index

INTERNATIONAL PERSPECTIVES ON ADULT AND
CONTINUING EDUCATION

Edited by Peter Jarvis
Consultant Editors: Chris Duke and Ettore Gelpi

CRAVEN COLLEGE

North Yorks BD23 1JY